Moody's Tale

JAMES BELL MOODY

ETT IMPRINT

Exile Bay

This edition published by ETT Imprint, Exile Bay 2018

Compiled by Tom Thompson from texts, photographs and
captions by James Moody as presented to Ion Idriess to create
Horrie the Wog Dog.

ETT IMPRINT
PO Box R1906
Royal Exchange NSW 1225 Australia

ISBN   978-1-925706-58-1 (paper)
ISBN   978-1-925706-59-8 (ebook)

Design by Hanna Gotlieb

Cover: Horrie sings to the accompaniment of a mouth organ,
Palestine 1941, hand-coloured by James Moody

CONTENTS

Trooper James Bell Moody

INTRODUCTION

Private James Bell Moody (VX13091) was a stalwart member of the 2/1st Machine Gun Battalion. While serving in Egypt he found a local dog which the unit named Horrie served for eighteen months as a willing mascot for the unit, known as the Rebels, in Egypt, Greece, Crete, Palestine and Syria. Horrie survived aerial bombardment and the sinking of their transport ship *Costa Rica.*

All that despite Routine Orders in June 1941 that stated: "The practise of keeping dogs and other pets is to cease. Commanders will ensure that personnel who already have pets dispose of them forthwith." The Rebels were very determined to bring Horrie home and on April 1st 1942, Moody brought home his dog Horrie from war inside his army pack on the transport *USS West Point*, and moved in with his father at 28 Meadow Street, East St Kilda.

After serving together surviving the sinking of their transport ship *Costa Rica*, Moody decided to tell Horrie's story with his mates of the 2/1st Machine Gun Battalion for possible publication, using his water-logged diaries as a starting poiint. However, he was soon frustrated with the quiet life in the Victoria Barracks, and went Absent Without Leave, with his friend Don Gill, who both embarked for service in New Guinea with the 2/7th Australian Infantry Battalion on 2nd November 1942.

Meanwhile the rest of the Machine Gun company arrived in New Guinea by January 1943. It was while "serving" in the army in New Guinea that Moody began his first Tale, an 18,000 word manuscript; and rejoined his old unit from "illegal absence" on January 10 1943. He went AWL again from April 15 through to the 28th, and was punished with a loss of pay. Undeterred, and keen for action, Moody and Gill left Duntroon on May 4 to Brisbane, where they were interviewed by Smith's Weekly and then on to Port Moresby, where they rejoined the 2/7th Infantry. On May 25 1943, Moody was fined 100/- for boarding a Transport without permission.

As *Smith's Weekly* noted:

Tired of sitting and waiting, they decided to go out in search of the enemy. So they walked out of camp and made their way to Brisbane. Instead of having a stolen holiday however, they walked into a Brisbane Camp and attached themselves to a unit that was soon to leave for New Guinea. On sailing day they boarded the transport as numbers of a fatigue party and secreted themselves on the ship until well out to sea and then reported to the O.C. (Officer in Command).

The Colonel, at a loss as to what to do with them, decided to take them temporarily on strength, until he could communicate with their own commander. Result was the men saw service at Milne Bay and on duty with jungle patrols...

On June 11 Moody applied to Major Dunkley for a transfer to the 2/7th, and was advised that the application must be submitted to the parent unit. Captain Reginald Dixon wrote to Moody on that day stating that "he does recall having two stowaways on his hands for disposal. However, we would be most happy to have you back with the unit – this time for keeps – only wish you could have been with us during the flap. I'm sure you would have enjoyed it."

Dixon and Dunkley was only too happy to take Moody on, but his old Unit felt otherwise, and Moody sent his Tale to Angus and Robertson, with several photographs of Horrie in action.

At Angus & Robertson publishers in Sydney, Ion Idriess was a constant visitor, having completed five of the six book Australian Guerrilla Series, all published in 1942. His classics like *The Cattle King, Drums of Mer, Flynn of the Inland, Forty Fathoms Deep, Gold Dust and Ashes and Lasseter's Last Ride, Men of the Jungle,* and *Over the Range* all reprinted that year. In 1943, most of these also reprinted, as well as his1941 title *The Great Boomerang*. While Idriess was working on *The Scout*, Walter Cousins of Angus and Robertson gave the Moody manuscript to Idriess, as he had been a Light Horseman in the Middle East in 1917. That month, Idriess wrote to Moody suggesting a collaboration to "make a book" of it:

There undoubtedly is partial material for a good dog book in the M.S. Unfortunately the material is not sufficient for a real book... our problem is to find material for a further 40,000 concentrated words at least. I have endeavoured to solve this by writing you a host of questions... By the time you've got to the end you'll be surprised at how much more you know of Horrie than you previously thought you did. Then go over the questions again, and write the answers out fully for me.

Moody agreed and Idriess wrote up the 63 Questions herein to help make the book take shape. "Your questions have simplified my task very considerably," Moody wrote back to Idriess on July 5 from New Guinea, adding "Perhaps I had better explain why this MS appears so disjointed and incomplete. I collected a very considerable set of photos whilst away from Aussie with this unit, and as so many included Horrie taken in various countries, I picked out roughly about 50 and connected them up more or less with the MS."

He mentioned how censorship at the time, and a lack of permissions forced him to leave out names, including ship names, and preferred not to mention his recent drama to the noted author: "Horrie is at my Dad's home in Melbourne, 28 Meadow Street, St Kilda... I am sorry I am not home & able to take him to you in Sydney... Cheerio and thanks for the confidence."

Thus Moody's first Tale herein closes with these lines:

After some eighteen months service with the A.I.F., the little wog-dog has been honourably discharged and today he enjoys he comfort and happiness of a well-cared for suburban dog. He has grown fat in his new found home and spends many hours lazing and sleeping in the sun...

In July, Idriess received a letter from Moody's father noting that Jack had now all the photos he required, while Moody's own post to Idriess, dated July 27: "I am forwarding the enclosed 124 pages on the instalment plan, it being rather inconvenient for me to keep it until I have answered all your questions."

By August 10, Moody writes to Jack: "I trust you will be able to extract a little more meat from this final instalment. I have kept a duplicate of the 364 pages posted to you in case they go astray in transit." He also notes that more photographs are with his father.

Moody Snr wrote to Jack on August 27 saying that he had now received his son's Horrie notes in 2 parcels, as "he had to lighten his pack of everything not wanted on the voyage... the little dog is A.1 & anxiously waiting for me to post this letter, he usually carries "Smith's Weekly" which I post regularly to Jim I have tried him with letters but the effort is not so good, especially if he meets any of his doggie friends enroute."

It is these 364 hand-written pages that make up Moody's second tale, published here for the first time as The Story of Corporal Horrie. Moody has written the work in good faith, with no monetary intent, as he has yet to get a contract with the publishers.

A last flurry of activity stopped with Moody's letter of September 24: "I think you now have all the help that I am able to give you, so am hoping you will be able to finish the job in your own style, and manner in which you think it best. Sorry the eventual publication seems rather distant, but I guess it can't be helped..."

Moody's Machine Gun unit was withdrawn from New Guinea in February 1944, and Moody was back in Australia on 20 February. Home on leave he notes in his letter to Idriess of 28 February that he will be in Sydney around March 20. After all this time, Moody was sighted at Angus & Robertson and they formally contracted with Idriess and Moody on April 11 1944, with both men to share royalties.

Moody's only problem was that he missed the draft for his unit who had left Sydney by train for Tenterfield that same day. Preferring to go back to fight in New Guinea with the 7th Battalion he found they had departed and he was once again declared an Illegal Absentee for the period ending 23 October 1944, and was docked 188 days pay.

Moody Snr wrote to Idriess on April 28, enclosing negatives of the "snaps of Horrie… some of these I think are of Horrie's mate Imshee & also one with her." 1944 was already a big year for Idriess, with two new books out – The Silent Service, with Torpedo Man Jones, and Onward Australia: Developing A Continent. That year *The Cattle King, The Desert Column, Drums of Mer, Gold Dust and Ashes, The Great Boomerang, The Great Trek, Headhunters of the Coral Sea, Lightning Ridge, Madman's Island,* and *Prospecting for Gold* all reprinted.

Moody was finally discharged from the Army on February 5, 1945 and Moody picked up Horrie from his father at St Kilda, and went by rail to Don Gill's home at 28 Silver Street, St Peters. On February 12 1945, the *Sydney Sun* published the first photograph of Horrie with Moody, and an article 'Horrie Embarks on Life of Peace'. This prompted enquiries by Mr Wardle, the Director of Veterinary Hygiene, Department of Health, who wrote to his counterparts in NSW and Victoria on February 14th referring to a similar story in the *Daily Telegraph* the day before, where it is noted that Horrie has been in Australia for several years and has a clean bill of health:

If the facts are as stated, there is no doubt that the dog has become past all risk, but there would be no reason why we cannot take action for a contravention of the Quarantine Act, and if the the facts gleaned reveal that Section 68 of the Act have been contravened, the dog could be seized and placed in a Quarantine Station pending a decision as to its disposal.

This will be the last time Wardle contemplated "that the dog has become past all risk", and from this point on he only seeks to marginal-

Ion Idriess meets Horrie 1945.

ise and threaten Moody. On February 16th he writes to the Department of the Army that "During March and April (1942) there were 19 vessels carrying troops and on which were animal mascots, mainly dogs. 21 dogs, 17 monkeys, 1 cat, 1 rabbit, 1 pigeon, 1 goose, 1 duck, 3 squirrels and 1 mongoose were destroyed, so it is quite possible that a small number of animals were surreptitiously landed... You will see from this that our Quarantine Officers are on the job."

Suddenly, both Moody and Horrie are in serious trouble.

Idriess then met Horrie at St Peters and photographs of this event begin appearing in newspapers in March 1945. The completed galley proofs were then sent by Mr Cousins at A & R to Mr Wardle on March 2, requesting Horrie's reprieve:

The dog went through the Greece and Crete campaigns with the soldiers and the two ships he travelled on to Greece and back from Crete were both torpedoed, but the dog's life was saved. I understand the dog has been three years in Australia and do hope that his life may be spared.

Jim Moody also made admissions to Mr Wardle on March 2, taking full responsibility for smuggling Horrie into Australia. He outlined Horrie's time in the Middle East with his unit, and that he did not declare the dog on his arrival and he would be destroyed. He mentions that Idriess has written a book about Horrie, and that he has offered his services to the Red Cross, and this was gratefully received. Moody is quite prepared to take any penalty himself, he simply wants to save the dog:

I do not wish to appear flagrant, but I would like to point out that it would be comparatively easy matter for me to have kept the dog's presence in Australia a secret, but by doing so I would be denying the Red Cross a helpful servant.

Moody was forced to pass over the dog to the Abbotsford Quarantine Centre on March 6 and telegrammed Mr Wardle asking for a reprieve on March 9, only to receive an ugly hand-written response: "Illegal entry of dog–owner J.B. Moody... You are advised that, by discretion of the Minister, the dog is to be disposed of by destruction and steps should be taken to have this carried out at once... (also) with reference to launching a prosecution against the person who illegally imported the dog. Approval has been obtained to prosecute."

Despite his clean bill of health, a Seizure Form to destroy an "Egyptian Terrier" was issued on March 12, and at 4pm that day, the dog was destroyed under Section 68 and Regulation 50 of the Quarantine Act. Poor Moody was given only five minutes notice of the event. The next day, Mr Cumpston, the Director-General of Health, replied to Moody's letter of March 2 in the harshest terms. Referring to "the incident of the dog owned by you which was illegally imported into Australia in March 1942...my Minister has decreed that the dog shall be destroyed. It is apparent that in illegally importing the dog, you showed an absolute disregard for the welfare of other animals and the human population of your home country..."

Wardle also wrote to Angus & Robertson March 13, acknowledging proofs of the "Wog-Dog" book, declaring that "I'm afraid I fail to appreciate the story and surprise is expressed that your firm would countenance a publication that records a deliberate breach of the law."

Idriess rewrote the ending of their book with Horrie's epitaph:

Well, Horrie little fellow, your reward was death. You who deserved a nation's plaudits, sleep in peace. Among Australia's war heroes, we shall remember you.

Letters from readers critical of the Government action, and animal lovers Australia-wide, bombarded the press, and the press complained that Horrie was "officially murdered", all this well before A & R's publication in June of *Horrie the Wog-Dog*. The book was also published in America that month as *Dog of the Desert* by Bobbs-Merrill. Reviews were uniformly good, even in America where the *Kirkus Review* wrote of it:

The true story of Horrie the Wog-Dog who was adopted by the Australian Signal Platoon of the M/G Battalion, in spite of all rules against keeping pets, and how Horrie not only won his stripes as a valuable addition to the group but had the further distinction of being smuggled into Australia on their return. The Wog-Dog was sneaked into Greece, went through the evacuation, carried messages as well as proving a dependable warning against air attacks. He went to Syria and Palestine, never learning to tolerate Arabs, -- he suffered cold and sickness, he fell in love with Ishmi, he was bombed off his ship and he never once was found during all necessary cover-up traveling. A story for all dog lovers, in spite of heavy Australian slang and style, of a dinkum Aussie who was kept, protected and loved by dinkum Aussies. Sentimentality over canines seldom misses fire.

Wardle as "Chief Vet in Canberra" found himself the subject of many strongly worded letters and requested a legal opinion on the possibility that the published letters critical of his actions could be construed as defamatory or libellous. Mr K.C. Waugh for the Crown Solicitor's Office in Canberra, however, thought otherwise and advised the Attorney General on July 25th:

.. any technical success which attended libel proceedings would do little or nothing to justify the departmental action of destroying the dog in the eyes of those members of the public who criticised it, but would only serve to advertise the matter afresh... In my opinion, therefore, no good purpose would be served by instituting libel proceedings against the writers of the letters in question.

The first print run in Australia was a large one, 10,000 copies, and these were exhausted by 1948 when A & R offered to buy out Moody's right and interest in Horrie, which Moody agreed to for 142 pounds

Several people have recently publicly claimed that Horrie wasn't euthanised at all in March 1945, and that Moody substituted another dog in his place. In 2002 Norma Allen told author Anthony Hill that she believed this, and that Moody told her that with Horrie's seizure imminent, he had searched the Sydney pounds until he found a similar dog that he bought for "five-bob". It was this dog Jim said he gave up to the authorities and it was destroyed in place of Horrie. According to this (happier) story Moody and the Rebels had the last laugh on authority. Horrie was said to have been whisked away to a farm near Corryong in northern Victoria. He was said to have lived his life there and sired many puppies. Hill's fine book *Animal Heroes* (Penguin, 2005), outlines this equally controversial story, and one of Moody's mates from his original Battalion, Brian Featherstone is noted in the *Age* (April 25 2008) as supporting the dog-substitute story.

However, it seems unusual that Moody kept this fact from his father Henry, who wrote him in April 1945:

I saw Mr Wilson again & he also read yr letter of 11ᵗʰ apparently they also were concerned over the way Horrie had been done to death and asked me to let him know what the contents of your confirming letter were as I had not then received. He seemed to expect that the Syd R.S.L. would be taking the matter up. Whatever happens, Jim I want you to keep away from any active part in it. You have nothing to blame yourself for. You did a splendid job for the little dog while he was alive& don't blame yourself for what happened thro' trusting to the honour & decency of men who apparently did not possess those virtues & consequently could not realise what that dog represented to the chaps who had been in the fighting. It is not possible for a backside hero sitting in a safe & cushy job to realise it. Nothing of note has happened here ... all the rest of the family appear well but very sad over the death of the little hero dog. Cheerio, eh Jim and do not go brooding over this business and remember please that whatever happens I want you to keep out of it as no doubt you will be a marked man for some time & if any lawlessness occurred you would probably be framed for it.

Another close friend of Moody, Captain Jim Hewitt wrote him on 6 April 45: "Dear Jim, At last the silence is broken – but then the death of Horrie would break anything ... I take particular pride in what little I did to help getting him home. The bastards." Why would Moody keep the substitution story from Jim Hewitt?

There is no doubt, however, that Moody was hurt by the public outcry, and the official response to his simple concern for a man's best friend. Perhaps Jim Moody decided later in life to give up an alternate tale, to soothe a few close friends and family. Perhaps such a story would give solace to those who had learnt to love Horrie through Moody's own wonderful photographs of the gallant little dog in "action". Or perhaps it was a secret only shared among a few of his trusted Rebels… Within *Moody's Tale* we can now see the honesty and humour of battle stripped bare, surrounded by his many fine portraits of Horrie; a tonic for the besieged desert troops. Thanks to James Bell Moody, Horrie lives on for us all.

Tom Thompson
Exile Bay

Moody's Tale

What happened to "Horrie" the little wog-dog? So many have asked this question that I have decided to try and tell everyone that cares to read this narrative something of the little dog's adventures from the time he first joined the A.I.F. in the Middle East.

You will probably wonder how he came by the name of Horrie the Wog-Dog. However, I had better try and start at the beginning,

At about the beginning of March 1941 we were camped at a place called Ikingi Mariut some twenty miles from Alexandria, Egypt, it was a very uninteresting place on the fringe of the Western Desert, nothing but sand and the occasional humble camp of the wandering desert Bediun met the eye.

The Beduins in this area were extremely poor although proud and friendly to Australian soldiers, many of the Beduin children wore disgarded "giggle suits" they had. been given to them by soldiers. Unlike the Arab from the native quarters of Alexandria these Beduin children would not ask for "backsheesh" (give me something) consequently they were popular with the troops who. were sorely pestered by the "backsheesh" urchins. The novelty of the East soon wore out and we became familiar with the custom of the Nile.

Amusement at Ikingi was mostly of our own making although we possessed if not boasted of a picture theatre.

Some fifteen odd miles from where we were camped there were some interesting old ruins and many of us spent our leisure hours exploring these ancient ruins, no one seemed to know much of the history of these ruins but it had obviously been a Roman City probably dating back to the time of Augustus in 554. There were still to be seen the remains of a marble palace which bore the unmistakable alias of Roman workmanship, these interesting ruins were usually referred to as the Lost City and they were being excavated during the time we were in that vicinity. Time and the moving sand of the desert had covered the ruins and much was still hidden from the eye. However, the entrance to what appeared to be a tomb bad been uncovered from a hill of sand and it was here that one of the boys discovered a skull, its owner long since dead had ceased to take an interest in life by receiving a blow on the head that had made a hole about the size of a penny. However, in spite of his or her untimely ending the skull had a decided grin and some wag suggested it would make a fine mascot so it was adopted by the platoon and given the name of "'Erb".

'Erb was given pride of place over the door of our tent and his perpetual grin did much to keep our sense of humour during the monotony of camp life and the numerous battalion parades. Shortly after the advent of 'Erb, the little wog-dog arrived and he was given the name of "Horrie".

His age was about six months when we found him, and he was completely lost and trying very hard to satisfy his puppy appetite by catching lizards that darted from rock to rock. The little pup seemed happy enough in his work as we stood watching him, but his efforts were not meeting with much success so I decided to give him a hand by moving a rock under which a particularly fat lizard bad evaded him. When he realised my intention his little stub tail wagged furiously, and as I moved the rock he darted in to the kill only to finish up with a mouthful of sand while the elusive lizard scurried under another rock. Horrie quickly followed with a yelp of anger, then turned to me with such a look of determination that I did not have the heart to laugh at him. I suggested that it might be a good idea if' he came back to the camp for a feed, at least the meat does not move as quickly as a lizard and there is not quite as much sand with it, so Horrie thought it may be a good idea. Little did I think then that it was the beginning of an adventure that few, if any, other dog has had in the space of fifteen months. The name "Wog" was given to the Arabs by the Australian soldiers. The Arab interpretation of "Wog" was "Worthy Oriental Gentleman", but I doubt if that was what the Australian soldiers had in mind about the "Orange" and "eggs is cook" vendor.

The Wog-dog's first meal in camp gave us some idea as to the identification of its past owner, for although the plate of meat that was offered to him should have been interesting enough, that is from a dog's point of view, he just sniffed it and promptly started to cover it over with sand, using his nose as a shovel. Some of the lads said that you could scarcely blame him, but as he was obviously hungry I was at a loss to know just how to feed him, keeping lizards up to him would certainly be a full-time job. However, one bright spark suggested perhaps he may be an Italian dog, so we tempted him with another plate of meat, this time lightly covered with olive oil. It was exactly what he needed, and the little wog-dog made short work of the second offering. On the outskirts of the Maruit area there were quite a few palatial homes, most of which were built after the style of a Roman castle. These homes were used mostly by wealthy Italians as week-end homes.

As Horrie, even when a small pup showed a very strong dislike for Arabs it seemed reasonably certain that he had belonged to one of the Italian Mariut residents, and had been left to his fate when the Italians were interned. Another reason was that his tail had been docked. The Arabs do not favour this whereas the Italians do, although this seems strange as they certainly favour the tail between the legs. However, this supposition may or may not be correct, but the fact remains that Horrie was well and truly lost when we found him, and as he was as fine as a four-penny rabbit, he had probably had a very miserable time prior to his joining the A.I.F.

The very important business of a good feed being over, a close examination suggested that next on the list should be a bath, as Horrie was sporting far more fleas than we were. Very soon a kerosene tin, warm water and lifebuoy soap appeared, and Horrie if not enjoyed, experienced what was probably his first bath. He did not violently object to the bath but when it was over he considered that he was quite entitled to make himself at home inside our tent.

No-one objected, but I noticed that several of the lads put their spare socks etc. out of reach. This proved to be a very good idea as it was not long before it became a common sight to see one of the boys legging it around the camp after the wog-dog, in an effort to try and regain some small part of his personal attire. Discretion being better than valour I usually managed to evacuate the tent before the irate owner of the missing sock returned, usually followed by Horrie, who kept a safe and annoying distance, while 'Erb' s grin from the door of the tent never seemed to improve matters much. Horrie when tired of this play would return the sock to me with a look that said "You take it back, I'm not game." Scolding made no difference to him, in fact he took this as praise for his ability to get into mischief, but in spite of his pranks he quickly became very popular with the boys and as accepted was part of the show. A bed was provided for him in the middle of the tent. It was constructed of a few pieces of board scrounged from the Q store and filled with straw. He was very pleased with it, and during the heat of the day spent many hours reclining in his box and at the same time keeping an eye on the door of the hut. His distrust of the Arabs grew as the days passed, and it was impossible for an Arab to approach within smelling distance from the tent, (about fifty yards with the wind in your favour).

Horrie proved a great asset in this respect, and it was quite safe to leave washing on the tent ropes overnight, providing it was out of the wog-dog's reach, but even in this case the garments did not disappear, they were merely torn into small pieces, and as they would probably have been pinched if it had not been for Horrie, nobody had room to complain.

The nights in Egypt were very cold, and it did not take Horrie long to find that the foot of my bed was warmer than his box. Shortly after lights out he would quietly settle himself on the bed, but the slightest movement on my part would send him back to his box to wait until I had settled down again. However, the morning always found him in his box, looking very innocent and eager to show his approval of everyone who spoke to him by wagging his tail in no uncertain manner. The little wog-dog dearly loved parades, and he would invariably accompany the inspecting Officer through the ranks, after the inspection he would take up position in front of the platoon but usually facing the troops instead or the front. He accompanied us on route marches also, and considered himself most important. It was comical to watch him leading the column, tail very erect and growling at anything and everything we passed, then looking up at us for approval. It was amazing the miles his little legs could cover before becoming tired. When he reached this point he would gradually drop back until someone picked him up and carried him for a spell, even then he never lost interest in the surroundings, and he always had a growl ready for a reply to the inevitable cry of "backsheesh" from the Arab urchins who seemed to appear from nowhere when the troops stopped for a smoke. Watermelons and oranges were offered from grubby little hands, and in some cases sweets were for sale. Also, although the vendors claimed that the goods were "very clean", "very sweet," "very hygiene," they were in fact the very opposite. It appeared as though some effort had been made to teach the Arabs something about hygiene. However, they had accepted it more as a joke than anything serious, although they were always anxious to help the sale of any article by claiming it as "very hygiene."

Cheerful little blighters, these Arab urchins, in spite of their appalling poverty and miserable existence, but they were intelligent, good humoured, and surprisingly quick to pick up some of the Australian slang phrases, especially when they found that it helped the sale of their goods to be able to backchat the soldiers with their own phrases. One bright little chap caused a roar of laughter when after watching Horrie complete his toilet by scratching sand in the approved doggie manner, exclaimed: "Very sanitary," while another little chap of about five years of age quickly fol-lowed up with "Wouldn't it?" Needless to say these bright lads received a just reward in the form of a few mils from the boys.

As the days passed the little wog-dog gradually superseded 'Erb and finally 'Erb was taken from his post and put out of sight and forgotten, but by this time the name "Horrie" had caught on and has stuck to the little dog to this day. After the weary monotonous months in the desert a move of any description would have been welcome, but the question soon arose, "What about Horrie?" We had all become so attached to the little pup by this time that it was out of the question to leave him behind.

At the same time we realised that it would be no easy matter to smuggle him aboard. Having definitely decided to give it a fly, next came the question "how?" Inside a sea-kit bag was the answer so I distributed the contents of my sea-kit bag among the boys, and gave Horrie a try-out. He realised that it was for a good cause, and did not object. We improved things a little for him by cutting a small hole large enough for his head in the side of the bag. A few practice runs around the camp and he became quite used to his new method of travelling, although his intense interest in everything was a bit of a worry, as even from his uncomfortable position, he could not supress a growl if he happened to see an Arab. No amount of scolding or coaxing would cure him of his disapproval of strangers, and he gave us a very bad moment while we were waiting on the wharf to embark for Greece. At last the great day came, and Horrie, displaying a new collar on which the battalion colour patch was sewn, was popped into the sea-kit bag. The inspection, which was not too close as far as I was concerned being over, we moved off on our trek to the Ikingi-Maruit railway station. Fortunately before we had travelled far I was able to pass the wog-dog to one of the boys who was going to the station in an army truck, and as we were carrying all our gear the march proved a very solid one. Horrie was lucky that he did not do the trip in the sea-kit bag.

Arriving eventually at the station, I found the pup tied to a tree a discreet distance away from the station. He was particularly pleased to see me and he probably had been wondering what was going to become of him. Any doubts he had in his doggie mind about being left, were soon dispelled, and once again he suffered the indignity of a Xmas turkey in a bag.

Once aboard the train it was possible to let him out again, and he spent most of the trip looking out of the train window in an effort to find something to growl at, anything at all would do, but Arabs received special attention.

The critical moment came when we reached the wharf at Alexandria, filing out of the train we formed up in three ranks for the final roll-call and it was at this moment that the wog-dog spotted some Arab workmen on the wharf. Prior to this moment, Horrie's disapproval of Arabs took the form of a growl, but this time it was a very definite bark, There was complete silence for a moment, then a few chuckles from the ranks. I managed to get the wog-dog's head inside the bag but although the barking stopped, the growl started. Looking as innocent as possible but with a thumping chest I cast an eye in the direction of the Officers, only to find discreet smiles. It was apparent that Horrie during his stay at camp had made many friends.

The first hurdle being more or less safely negotiated, made me a little more careful about the second, which I imagined would be the worst, that being the ship's crew. However I was soon to find out the typical good-fellowship of the British Navy man. We eventually parked ourselves in the aft hold and once again Horrie was able to stretch his little legs, this could have been disastrous also, as a few moments after he was let out one of the boys called "Yow!" I made a frantic effort to get him back into the bag, but Horrie did not feel disposed to give up his newly found freedom so soon, and the stern and was proved stubborn. The cause of the "Yow"' call turned out to be in the form of a Tommy sailor who, unknown to me was watching my effort to get to the stern and out of sight.

"It's O.K. digger. You can let him out. We've got one also. " These reassuring words were the signal for Horrie's public appearance, and the thumping in my chest to cease. The ship's crew possessed a dog very similar in all respects to Horrie. They were undoubtedly the same breed, except for the fact that Horrie had a stub tail, it would have been difficult for a stranger to tell them apart. The ship's dog rejoiced in the name of "Ben" , this being short for Benghazi, where the crew had picked him up after the Italians had been driven out during the big push early in 1941. Like Horrie, Ben had also been left to fend for himself, his previous master had probably been far too worried about himself to bother about the dog. However, Ben was now in good hands and seemed quite contented with the hazardous life on the sea.

The first night we spent below deck, and it was not till we were well out to sea the following day that the wog-dog put in appearance on deck. Everything must have seemed very strange to him and he showed an intense interest in everything, particularly the water which he very cautiously watched by putting his head through the rails on the side of the ship, and at the same time inclining his body inwards. As the usual growl seemed to make no difference to the view of the Mediterranean, he turned his attention to the troops, everyone received a sniff, a wag of approval and an invitation for a romp around the deck. One of the ship's crew produced Ben and the two wog-dogs soon became firm friends. Ben who was by this time an old sailor had a decided advantage over Horrie during their romps on deck, the ship being on some 3000 tons, rolled considerably and Horrie having not yet found his sea legs was never able to catch Ben during the game which appeared to be "Catch me if you can."

Becoming tired after this game Ben escorted Horrie on a tour of inspection which must have included a visit to the ship's galley for when Horrie next put in an appearance, he had in his mouth a good size bone. His luck was in as at this stage of the game we had only bully beef to offer him and he had not as yet been introduced to hard rations.

Soon after midday on the first day out from Alex., it started to blow up a bit rough and it was not long before Horrie started to lose interest in the fun and games. I have often heard the expression "as sick as dog" but had never realised just how miserable this condition is until the little wog-dog became sea-sick. Having selected a quiet place to lie down and die myself, Horrie joined me and I doubt if there were ever a more miserable pair. Horrie lay with his chin on the deck and his little legs stretched out fore and aft, and for hours his eyes never left my face. Obviously he expected me to do something to stop the ship from rolling, but the only effort I was able to make was to give my contribution to the fishes.

The following morning proved to be much calmer and Ben did everything in his doggie power to coax Horrie to play but the little wog-dog was convalescent and could not be persuaded to play. He was quite contented to watch with envious eyes the pranks of the old sea-dog.

Being now into the danger zone, everyone was wearing their life jackets, so we made one for the wog-dog. It was constructed of a few pieces of cork strapped to his sides, and back with a two-inch bandage, but Horrie thought it unnecessary and with the help of Ben soon removed it.

Late in the afternoon we passed several small islands, so we guessed that we were nearing our destination and the end of a rough but uneventful trip. At about 6pm we sailed into Port Piraeus, the port for Athens. It was a beautiful harbour, numerous small islands and bays but the most pleasing sight of all was the green foliage on the shore.

The trees, bracken fern, green grass and the clean white houses that dotted the shore were a sight that we had sorely missed in the desert, which in comparison boasted only of sun, sand and smells.

Horrie managed to find a view point between the legs of the troops that lined the side of the ship and the sight of land and particularly the trees must have gladdened his stout little heart. Some little time later we anchored a few hundred yards from the shore and the journey by ship was over.

After getting our gear together we formed up on deck and once again the wog-dog was popped out of sight inside the sea-kit bag. Ben, who thought it was a new sort of game, made several playful nips at the bottom end of the bag, while Horrie voiced his disapproval of this unfairness from the hole in the side, while all the time I was endeavouring to "stand at ease" and pay attention. Horrie, running true to form was determined to bark his way off the ship just as he had barked his way on. Ben joined in the chorus and the racket was considerably louder than the voice of the O.C. who gave us disembarkation orders without, as it would seem, even knowing that the wog-dog was on board. Small lighters came alongside to take us off the ship, a gangway was lowered and we started to disembark.

From the lower end of the gangway to the small craft there was a drop of about three feet, and consequently the Greeks on the lighter helped the troops by taking all kit bags, and giving the boys more freedom to make the jump. Seeing that I would have no option about handing my sea kit to the Greek I called to one of the boys to keep an eye on it and the bag containing the wog-dog passed into the hands of the helpful Greek The very obvious thing happened. Horrie started to wriggle and the Greek helper, taken completely by surprise, muttered something in Greek and dropped the bag very smartly. Naturally Horrie objected to this rough handling and the wriggling bag started to growl. Before the Greeks had time to realise what it was all about I was able to pick up the bag and disappear among the troops on the lighter.

Although I doubt if a search would have been made for the dog, the Air Raid warning from the ship which was sounded at that moment, dispelled any fear on that account.

Amid much gesticulation on the part of the Greeks, we made a very erratic course to a small pier, eventually got ashore, and I was able to let Horrie out of the bag.

Shortly after getting ashore the Ack-Ack defence guns went into action. This was the wog-dog's first experience of gun fire. He lost all interest in the numerous trees that must have seemed like paradise to the dog from the desert, and quickly scampered back to me. I picked him up and carrying him under my arm, joined the boys who had sought shelter in a drain along-side the road. Horrie was well and truly scared and was trembling like a leaf. But it did not take very long to soothe him. We sat in the drain and watched the raid that seemed to be directed mostly against the ships that were in the harbour. It was a brilliant spectacle, numerous searchlights, tracer bullets from machine guns and red, yellow and green flaming onions from the ack-ack guns filled the sky, time and time again, the searchlights picked up the planes which, gleaming silver in the light, twisted, turned and dived in an effort to escape the bright beams, and often directed a burst of machine gun fire down the beam of the searchlight in vain hope of blotting out the light. As soon as the searchlights picked up a plane the flaming onions would start up from all points of the compass and as they appeared in a slowly moving stream of various colours it seemed more like "Henley on the Yarra" than an air raid on Port Piraeus.

The deep "whoompt" of a bomb exploding fairly close was the signal for Horrie to go into action and with hair bristling and tail erect he barked his disapproval of the Luftwaffe. Someone nearby panicked and shouted: "Keep the bloody dog quiet or they'll hear us." Although we had a fairly healthy respect for the German airmen, not many of us thought they were that good. However, to please all Horrie was stopped from barking but his growl showed that even if he was not allowed to loudly proclaim his disapproval of the luttwaffe, he could at least do his bit by growling.

After a delay of about thirty minutes we moved off again to a little Greek village named Daphney and camped there for the night. During the early hours of the morning several hostile aircraft flew low over the camp and dropped their eggs uncomfortably close. The earth shook and a shower of leaves fell on the tent roof from the trees among which we were camped. The wog-dog crept from the foot of my bed and buried his cold nose under my arm pit. Finding that he was not ejected he gained courage and once more started to growl.

The morning found us camped in a delightful spot, April sunshine, green crops, wines and fields of poppies met the eye, and the trees under which we were camped were good old Australian gums. This indeed seemed a country worth fighting for. During the morning numerous children invaded the camp and they were given tins of bully beef by the boys, much to their delight for it seemed a luxury to them. Meat of any kind was scarce then and the wog-dog bad his first meal of bully-beef. He certainly did not show the enthusiasm about it that the Greek kiddies did.

The following day we passed through Athens and we were greeted with cheers and flowers from the warm-hearted people of this lovely land, from the back of a truck Horrie watched with interest, tail wagging and an occasional bark of greeting to any dog that he saw. His interest in everything was amazing and it was Horrie that first drew our attention to a sight that was to us most unusual. As we passed through Laressa he spotteda stork perched on its huge nest high up on a church steeple. He was so concerned about it that we just had to see what all the noise was about.

The quaint white-washed houses, the Greek peasants in their colourful costumes and the stork presiding over all from his lofty perch on a church steeple made such a peaceful. scene that it was hard to realise that the black clouds of war were threatening this beautiful country.

The following day Horrie's method of travelling changed from truck to motor cycle. This was accomplished by putting him in the front of my greatcoat after first fastening a belt around the waist so he would not fall out. He kept his interest in the surroundings by putting his head out between two buttons, much to the amusement and delight of the Greek people whose attention he drew with his ever ready bark.

Horrie travelled many miles in this fashion and seemed to like it. I had only to sit on a motor-cycle and open the front of my coat and he would scramble up and make himself comfortable, but the moment I stopped, his scramble to get out never lacked in enthusiasm.

The following day we were getting nearer to the beautiful snow-topped Mount Olympus and the air became very cold. We managed to keep Horrie warm by cutting the heel and toe off a sock and putting the remainder over his body. He looked comical and uncomfortable, but he certainly appreciated the extra warmth judging by the tail wagging.

April 15th found us at the foot of Mount Olympus and enemy air-craft appeared in large numbers for the first time since the night we arrived at Port Piraeus.

Battalion H.Q. was established and the troops moved out to join the Anzac Corps which had withdrawn to the Olympus - Aliakmon line. The following day Horrie experienced dive bombing and machine gunning in real earnest at Servia Pass.

Rather than leave him at Br. H.Q. I took him with me during a dis-patch run to one of· our companies in position with two Australian and one New Zealand brigades. Had I suspected beforehand that it was to be a nightmare trip the little wog-dog would certainly have been left behind at the slightly more tenantable site of Battalion H.Q. German air reconnaissance proceeded and large flights of aircraft dive-bombed and machine gunned positions and road convoys. Spotters riding on the running board of trucks constantly scanned the sky and when the pres-ence of hostile aircraft was noticed the trucks jolted to a halt and the per-sonnel scattered for any kind of cover available on the side of the road.

The aircraft, mostly in flights of twenty-one would leisurely select a target and then down they came, siren screaming, accompanied by the larger scream of bombs, the sharp crack of small arms' fire from the men lying in the fields on the side of the road would be blotted out by the "whoompt" of exploding bombs. Having dropped their eggs the enemy aircraft would machine-gun the vicinity of the convoy before returning for another load of ammunition.

Horrie accompanied me during the first hectic run for cover and probably thought it a game till the scream of sirens and the detonation of bombs recalled to his memory the first air raid in Pireaus. However we went to ground together in a ploughed furrow and feeling about the size of Cheops pyramid, waited for the worst. When silence reigned supreme I lifted my head in time to see the others doing likewise. It looked funny to see numerous heads pop up from a seemingly inno-cent ploughed paddock. All eyes looked up at the receding planes and mostly everyone said the same thing: "Missed, you b....."

I picked up the wog-dog and directed his gaze at the planes. He caught on and started to growl, much to the amusement of the boys. From this moment Horrie became our best spotter, or perhaps I should say, "Plane Listener" for when we were occupying various positions he would always be the first to pick up the sound of aeroplanes. When this happened he would sit very erect with his ears cocked and a look of intense interest, then the growl would start.

At this stage of the game there were no planes wearing our gurnsey, we would take heed from Horrie and make for the nearest slit trench, always preceded by the wog-dog who would stop at the lip of the trench, look back to see if we were following, then with enough wags of the stumpy tail to say "good show these trenches" jump in and bark a warning for us to follow quickly. Horrie always received a pat for his warning and no-one ever laughed at him for we had found that he was very sensitive and would become offended if laughed at or made fun of. This sensitiveness of the wog-dogs became apparent one day when we were crossing a river. We found a tree that had fallen across the river and decided that it was our best means of crossing. However, one stream had previously covered the log but had receded leaving the log uncovered and very slippery. Horrie noted our intention to cross the log and promptly went first. When about half way across he slipped and into the cold stream he went. He swam to the opposite bank and scrambled out. It looked so funny that we all laughed. Horrie noted this and promptly advanced towards us over the log from the opposite side of the river. When once again about half way across he stopped, then barked to make sure we were all watching him, satisfied that we were he deliberately jumped into the stream and swam ashore. He made himself perfectly plain. He was trying to tell us that he did not fall in at all but did it on purpose. Such a gallant effort on Horrie's part could not go unrewarded and from then on those who knew him well would never dream of laughing at him unless he was obviously playing.

At about the 15th April we learnt that the title of the First Australian Corps had been changed to Anzac Corps. This recognition of the partnership in Greece was very popular with both the Australian and the New Zealand troops. At about the same time it was rumoured that our Greek Allies were in very bad shape and that the bulk of their forces on our left flank had collapsed. A few days later we passed through Larissa which presented a very difficult face to that which we had first seen. Larissa had been subjected to constant and heavy bombing and was a shambles. Gone were the friendly people who had cheered us as we passed through only a short time previously. Now, only a heap of stone was the church and high steeple where the stork had surveyed the peaceful view beneath him. The troops were strangely silent as we passed through.

As the withdrawal progressed the convoys in retreat became more congested and the road from Larissa to Lamia was choked with vehicles. When the withdrawal first commenced movement had been made only and as it was doubtful how long the enemy could be held by the small stopping force, it became necessary to move the endless convoy during the daylight hours. From daylight till dark the stretch of road between Larissa and Lamia received very violent air attacks and time and time again the slowly moving convoy had to halt and the personnel take cover off the road. Horrie, being wise in the way of attacking planes, never waited for me now, but scampered for cover of his own choice. He was quite aware that his little legs could carry him faster than my own could, but he would often stop to see if I was following until he heard the whine of bombs falling then it was every dog for himself. After the raid was over he came trotting back growling away to himself.

He gave me one very bad moment after a raid during which Horrie had selected his own funk hole. I whistled for him but he failed to return. Several bombs of a small calibre had fallen very close and we were showered earth and stones. Feeling sick I started off in the direction I had last seen him heading. However, a subdued bark answered my frantic whistle and I found him in an old slit trench. He had certainly found a better shelter than we had, but after getting into the trench he was unable to get out again without help. Horrie must have wondered what all the fuss was about as everyone wanted to pat him at once. Choice tit-bits such as army biscuits were offered to him in reckless abandon and the fact that the old trench had been used for other purposes did not mean a thing. Poor Horrie had to be cleaned with petrol, there being no water available for a very necessary spot of toilet.

The Luftwaffe bad played merry hell during the withdrawal to Thermopylae, the road was cratered by numerous bombing and everywhere along the road were overturned trucks and burnt-out vehicles. The main features in the Thermopylae position were the low coastal area along which rolled the road from Lamia to Volos, and the steep Bralos Pass through which ran the main road from Athens to the north. The strength of the Sixth Australian Division bad been appreciably weakened by battle casualties and as no reserve was available it became apparent that the fight on the mainland was drawing to a close. The Greek forces on the left had surrendered leaving a way open for the German forces to work into the rear of the Thermophlae position from Yannina.

April 25th, Anzac Day found us hidden among olive trees at a small village named Kaloni. All day long the Luftwaffe flew overhead searching for and machine gunning positions, during the day a few of us managed to secure some fowls. These we roasted and celebrated the day with our first good meal for a many a long day. Horrie probably enjoyed his share more than we did, for it was the first time that he had seen anything that resembled a bone since we landed in Greece.

During the night we moved again to Kalamata and it was here that I saw a sight that will remain forever in my memory. It was obvious that we were leaving Greece but the kind-heartedness of the genuine poor Greek villagers in this little village was brought home by the sight of and old men and women filling in bomb craters on the road so that we were able to continue without delay ordetouring. Vehicles had to be destroyed, blankets and goods were given to the villagers wherever possible, small treasured trifles of personal kit were destroyed so that the maximum amount of small arms and ammunition could be carried. At dusk we moved to the beach and waited for the Navy to take us off.

Sleep leave, begrimed and bitter men waited patiently in silence, each busy with his own thoughts. Would the overworked Navy make it? Each of us realised that a slip up now meant extermination or surrender as the end to a hopeless bitter struggle.

At about 1.30am lights blinked out at sea. Someone near me said: "Christ, they've made it!"and it was so. Before long destroyers came alongside a small wharf with the familiarity of a Sydney ferry pulling alongside Circular Quay. Without panic or fuss troops boarded the destroyers and were ferried out to waiting troop ships. As we watched the dim outline of Greece disappear our thoughts turned to the gallant friends we had left behind and each man was grim, tired but bitterly determined that this was not the true ending to the battle for Greece.

It was not necessary to conceal Horrie; and I carried him under my arm. The boys relieved me of some equipment so that I could scramble aboard the troopship and once again we were under way. Machine guns were mounted at vantage points then the troops curled up and slept in any space that offered room to lay down. Horrie also was dog tired and was sound asleep a few minutes after we bad found a place to sleep in.

At about 8 a.m. we were awakened by what sounded like the old push type motor car horn. Nobody seemed to know what it was for, but the sight of the Air Raid Red flag being hoisted told us the worst - after a few hours sleep and peace it was on again.

There were roughly about 4,000 troops aboard our ship and apart from the machine guns, almost every man had a rifle and each quickly found some place from whence he could fire. We were a small convoy of three troopships escorted by several destroyers and cruisers. The bark of A.A. guns from the escort followed by the greyish puffs of bursting A.A. shells in the sky first showed us the position of the attack-ing planes. One after the other they came down selecting the middle ship of the convoy as their target. Waterspouts caused by exploding bombs shot high into the air and the sky was filled with the puffs of A.A. shells. The sharp bark of small arms fire could plainly be heard above the din. The planes flattened out just above the mast of the ship and the flight of tracer bullets could be seen. One plane continued its dive and disappeared with a huge splash into the sea. A chorus of "You beaut!" came from the boys on our ship while the sound of cheering drifted over to us from the attacked ship.

We were selected by the next flight and the Bren guns on the fore-castle deck were first in action. Down they came, right into a hail of lead. The small arms fire was so intense and accurate that each plane deviated and the bombs fell close but harmlessly into the water. The next attack followed immediately. The racket was terrific. Everything that would fire was being used, even revolvers and anti-tank rifles. Some even say that the stokers were throwing lumps of coal up the funnel. Chips flew from the mast as the machine guns swung round to follow the flight of the planes and the wire rigging was frayed in many places where it had been nicked by bullets. Although he probably did not know it, the gamest man on the ship was the chap in the crows nest. The flight of tracer bullets could be seen passing horribly close to his precarious position, but nevertheless he was shouting and waving his arms in encouragement to the gunners below. The piano in the saloon started up and those who were unable to get a position on deck started to sing. A wild cheer marked the end of another plane. The little wog-dog showed no sign of fear but helped to swell the noise with his bark. I tied him up in a corner out of the way on the sun deck. He took a very poor view of being tied up, but it was for the best as the troops were far too busy to notice a small dog at their feet.

The centre ship was attacked again and a stick of three bombs exploded harmlessly close to her stern. She was blotted out of sight by a sheet of water for a moment and again a cheer went up as the waves subsided and she was seen to be still forging ahead steadily.

There was no let-up and hour after hour the planes attacked. By midday the bag of planes had mounted to five and all ships were still afloat. We accounted for the fifth plane and a Lucas lamp from the bridge of the centre ship signalled the following:

"Congratulations on the volume of small arms fire. Good show, keep it up."

But the end was near. At about 1.30 p.m. we were again the chosen one. By now the sun was well up and the planes taking advantage of this came down at us from out of the sun, making it hard for us to see them until they flattened out above the ship. The scream of a bomb falling very close was heard above the din then a terrific explosion rocked the ship. The vibration brought down some of the damaged rigging. A huge sheet of water was flung up over the port stern. We had zigged when we should have zagged. Fortunately for hundreds of troops the bomb missed the ship but fell so close that the damage was done. The engines stopped and the firing ceased. A strange silence fell over the ship. It was apparent that we were in serious trouble. The planes had disappeared, and the troops remained quietly at their posts. Soon a destroyer came alongside and the Captain asked through a megaphone: "What is the matter?"

The silence on the ship was broken by some wag answering: "We've run out of petrol."

A voice from the bridge of our ship supplied the correct answer.

"Ship badly holed. Six feet of water in the engine room and engine moved off its mounting."

Without any delay the destroyer called alongside to take off troops. Little boats were lowered and rafts thrown overboard. Some of the troops stripped and jumped over the side.

At the time we were hit I was on the forecastle deck and it was with considerable difficulty that I reached the spot where Horrie was tied up I managed to get there and found the wog-dog safe and sound, but looking a bit worried. I picked him up and made my way to the side of the ship which now had a considerable list to starboard. A destroyer came alongside and the troops started to scramble aboard. From the sun-deck of the troop-ship to the deck of the destroyer there was a drop of about twenty feet and ropes were thrown to the destroyer and the troops climbed down the ropes. This was no easy matter because the troopship had settled heavily and the small destroyer rose and fell with the swell making the descent by rope rather difficult. As I had discarded my overcoat I now had no place to put Horrie and leave my hands free. It seemed impossible to make the descent with Horrie under my arm leaving me with only one serviceable arm. There was only one thing to do, and I called to some or the boys on the destroyer "Catch my dog!" The ready answer came back: "O.K., let him go dig."

The poor pup sailed through the air to the eager hands waiting to catch him on the destroyer below. He twisted and turned in the air, but was caught by the boys below and he suffered only a bad fright. After gaining the deck of the destroyer, he was handed to me, wagging his tail furiously. So that he would be out of the way I put him into one of the lifeboats on the destroyer and then gave a hand to steady the ropes down which the troops were still descending.

Poor Horrie was yet to get another bad fright. Just in the nick of time I noticed that one of the life boats, partly launched on the troopship had slipped at one end and as the destroyer lifted in the swell the lifeboat in which Horrie had been placed came up directly under the lifeboat on the troopship. I snatched him out a few seconds before the two wooden boats met and smashed to pieces.

It was very close but the little wog-dog still managed to wag his tail and lick my hand. In less than thirty minutes all the troops had been taken off and the destroyers circled the stricken ship and picked up men from rafts, lifeboats and some who were in the water.

Fortunately the planes did not appear during the rescue and once again we were under way and bound for Crete. One of the British sailors produced some raw meat and offered it to Horrie, but the excitement of the past few hours had been too much and the pup had lost his appetite, but he still had a wag left for the sailors and troops who made a great fuss of him.

We reached Suda Bay, Crete, before the planes attacked again, As soon as we pulled alongside the wharf we scrambled off and raced for cover. Most of the small arms had been lost on the troopship and we were helpless. However, the barrage from the destroyers kept the planes up and they lost a golden opportunity of machine gunning the troops as they ran for cover.

The wog-dog was so pleased to get his feet on terra firma again that he did not race away on his own accord, but ran alongside me and showed his pleasure by jumping up every now and again on my legs.

We presented a sorry sight when we formed up again. Many were without boots and some almost naked. Some appeared to be half soldier and half sailor as they were wearing clothes that had been given to them by members of the destroyer's crew. We eventually reached a transit depot and were given a hot meal and a very welcome mug of tea. As I sat under an olive tree to eat our first good meal for many a long day, I heard someone call my name. I found the chap who was calling me and he said;

"I've got your dog here dig."

As I had left Horrie with some of my platoon only a few seconds ago I thought it must be a joke of some description, but he produced a dog that would have passed for Horrie by anyone that did not know him very well. This soldier had heard about Horrie and had rescued it from the troopship where it had apparently been a pet, thinking the dog was our mascot. He had looked after it and had intended to return the dog to us when he eventually located our platoon. As we did not see any of the ill-fated troopship's crew again, we were unable to return their pet to them, so we adopted the dog, and as it was a bitch, we named her "Horrietta."

Horrie and his girl-friend got along very well together, and when we moved off again after our meal, they trotted at the head of the column looking very important, and obviously very pleased to be on land again.

Eventually we established a camp of a kind near Cones. It was a delightful place among the olive trees and close to a small stream which we dammed and made a small swimming pool. The crystal-clear water came from the melting snows of the vague purple and white-capped mountains. Although the water was very cold we enjoyed a refreshing plunge and a wash and scrub after the grimy days in Greece.

Horrie and Horrietta also had a good wash, but I doubt it if they enjoyed as we did. During the first few days on Crete we were able to catch up with our sleep. After selecting a spot to sleep in the sun, Horrie, who now considered that my blanket was as much his as mine, joined me in peaceful oblivion.

The island of Crete lies across the eastern Mediterranean and is an alongate mountain mass some 170 miles long and ranging from 10 to 30 miles wide. There were numerous olive groves, barley fields and grape vines. Everywhere possible the land was cultivated, even on the side of the hills the frugal Cretan folk had levelled out the ground until it appeared like huge steps covered with a light green carpet of grape vines. The Cretan people are very friendly and although their island was not very well stocked with food they were always ready to offer such luxuries as fruit, eggs and wine, which was very welcome to us after our long period of hard rations. We made ourselves as comfortable as possible in one of the numerous olive groves, many of the olive trees were hollow, and with a little ingenuity these trees would become a moderately good camping place.

Horrie disappeared early one morning shortly after our arrival on Crete. At first we did not worry very much thinking that he had probably gone on a hunting trip of his own, and he became tired he would return. But as he had not returned by nightfall we became anxious. Horrietta had not accompanied him and when we started to whistle and call Horrie, she became very excited. We tried to make her follow Horrie's scent but this effort did not meet with any success. We searched all night for the wog-dog without result. Whenever a dog barked in the distance we set off in that direction but time and time again only to find a dog belonging to some Cretan. We returned to the site of our camp very tired and miserable. As we were moving to another part of the island that day it seemed as though our last chance to find Horrie was gone. We packed our few scanty belongings and were ready to move on again when we heard Horrie's familiar bark. He came streaking towards the olive grove towards us, then round and round he scampered as fast as his little legs could carry him. I have never seen a dog look so happy when he eventually stopped he wagged his little stumpy tail so hard that it seemed as though he would break his back. There was a length of rope attached to his collar and it had obviously been chewed through. The little wog-dog had apparently been tied up but fortunately whoever it was had used a rope and Horrie had been equal to the occasion and made good his escape. Had a chain been used Horrie probably would have been left behind in Crete.

The following day the Luftwaffe attacked the shipping in Suda Bay. Horrie, ever mindful of his experience in Greece scooted for cover but poor Horrietta trembled violently and was so scared that we decided it would be better if we could find a home for her with some Cretan family. This we eventually did, and the simple, friendly folk were so pleased with the dog that we felt reassured that the ship-wrecked pup would have a good home. It was fortunate that we found a home for her because as the days passed the food became very scarce and although each of us gave Horrie a portion of our rations, it was not nearly enough and Horrie lost quite a lot of weight. But in spite of this he was quite happy and contented with his lot. When we sat down to eat he would beset one after the other and ask for his portion in the very best manner, by sitting in front of the soldier and waiting patiently for a small piece of bully beef or Army biscuit that would always be offered to him.

A rather amusing incident happened one day when Don Gill and myself called in at what appeared to be the local store for a small village. This store seemed to have quite a large range of goods and we thought it just possible that they might have dog-biscuits which would have been very helpful to supplement the wog-dog's meagre rations. We took Horrie with us into the store and produced an Army biscuit pointed to the dog, then went through the motions of eating, but the Cretan store-keeper just smiled and shook his head. Determined to make ourselves understood we repeated the performance, whereas the store-keeper said: "Yes, I know what you mean, but I haven't any." We ail enjoyed the joke although it was at our expense. However we were able to buy the pup some milk which he put away in good time.

As the days passed there was a marked increase in the air activity of the Luftwaffe, but Horrie was now a seasoned warrior and took everything in his stride. He adapted himself to circumstances so well and so uncomplainingly that his show of guts did much to help lighten our own hardships.

After the evacuation from Greece a large proportion of British and Imperial forces landed on Crete with only their own personal arms, and many with no arms or equipment at all, owing to their transport having been sunk by air action. This created a situation with which the local resources were unable to cope and owing to this unfortunate fact, many troops were evacuated to Egypt before Crete finally passed into the hands of the ruthless, efficient Hun.

The day eventually arrived when Horrie was to take part in another evacuation. This time it was accomplished in an empty ammunition box. Everything went smoothly until "Stukas" dive-bombed the ship as we were embarking. The familiar "whoompt" of bombs bursting started Horrie growling again, but I managed to gain the gun-deck at the aft end of the ship and there was fortunate in finding a large canvas tarpaulin, and under this cover let the pup out of the box. It must have looked damn' silly to see me sitting up on the deck during the raid and talking to a small bulge in the canvas, but I had accomplished my purpose in getting the dog on board and I certainly was not going to spoil the effort by letting Horrie bark.

We suffered no damage by the raid, and when we were under way the little wog-dog was allowed out from his hiding place under the Tarpaulin.

We were aboard a cargo ship of some 10,000 tons and now bound for Port Said. The hatch covers had been removed and the troops relaxed either on deck or below, wherever they could find room. Fortunately we were able to remain on the gun-deck where it was possible to keep Horrie more or less out of sight, although once under way he was fairly safe.

At daylight we were in trouble again. The engine broke down and the ship just wallowed in the heavy swell. We were an absolute sitting shot for anything that came along. We watched another ship loaded with troops gradually disappear in the distance. However, a destroyer came alongside and once again we were told to stand by to abandon ship. Our luck turned, and soon after this order the welcome sound of the engine turning over broke the spell and we were again under way.

At about 9 a.m. we shared our last few tins of bully beef with Horrie. Water was scarce but with a little luck we hoped to reach Egypt again within the next two days. After a cold miserable night the warm morning sun was welcome and we dozed on the gun-deck. However, at about 11.45 a.m. the air raid alarm brought us back to reality. Shortly after the alarm we saw five planes flying at a great height. They appeared to have passed us by and we were waiting for their familiar trick of flying into the sun then coming down at us in a dive when we heard the scream of bombs falling. We crouched under the gun on deck, it being the only shelter offering. A stick of four bombs fell very close to the port side of the ship. Oily salt water was flung high into the air, then descends in a torrent on the deck. Shrapnel rattled against the side of the ship which almost looped the loop, but our luck held and we were still under way. The planes did not return and when we had sorted ourselves out I noticed that Horrie was limping. A close examination revealed that he had a small piece of shrapnel embedded under the skin on his shoulder. We managed to remove it with a knife blade. Horrie did not even whimper, but as I pinched the skin under the piece of metal while Don Gill removed it, he licked my hand and wagged his tail. Fortunately it was very slight and did not worry him nearly as much as it did us.

The remainder of the journey to Port Said was peaceful. I carried Horrie under my arm when we disembarked from the ship. It was not necessary to conceal him but the boys crowded around me and made it difficult for anyone to see the small white pup under my arm. Once aboard the train he was allowed the freedom that a crowded cattle truck can offer. The wound on his shoulder seemed to worry him a little so we took the field dressing off and enabled him to lick it. He soon forgot his trouble when he heard the voices of Arabs who were selling sweets to the lads in the trucks while we were waiting to move off. I lifted him up and let him see over the side of the truck. He immediately sighted the Arabs and showed by his barking that he had not forgotten them. Eventually we arrived at El Kantara on the Suez Canal, a huge receiving depot had been established here for the troops arriving back from Crete. We were given a very welcome change of under-clothing, tobacco and cigarettes, a hot meal and a refreshing shower, after which we continued our journey to Palestine where our home was to be for the next seven months.

Palestine at this time was well settled with Australian troops. Comfortable camps had been established early in 1940, However, the Holy Land was new to us who had been in England when Palestine became acquainted again with Australian Diggers.

We camped at first at a place named Dier Suneid some nine miles from Gaza, the scene of much fighting during the 1914-1918 world war. Dier Suneid was rather interesting during the first few weeks of our stay there, the yellow sand was contrasted by orange groves of beautiful green. These groves were hedged by cultivated cactus plants. The Arabs also wore more colourful gowns than those we had seen in Egypt. However, Horrie, who had completely recovered from his wound within a few days, still took a very poor view of the Worthy Oriental Gentlemen and he immediately placed himself on duty outside our tent as soon as we arrived. He certainly took his watch seriously and it was impossible for an Arab to approach our tent without having his flowing night-shirt-like gown torn by the wog-dog's sharp little teeth. Horrie, who now considered himself an old warrior was no longer contented to bark but now took the fight right to his enemy who invariably did the wrong thing and ran when spotted by Horrie. The little pup would always catch and bail the Arab up until one of us called him off. The Arab would usually say "No klefti, George,"(steal). "Kalb Musquise dog no good."

But in nine out of ten times it was because the dog was good that the Arab was "no klefti."

Quite close to our camp at Dier Suneid there was an Arab village,and being curious we decided to have a good look around. We were also anxious to try out a little Arabic that we had learnt from an impossible book known as "Arabic for one shilling." The dwelling places were constructed of mud brick walls and straw roofs. Each house has its own individual yard within the walls, separated from the single dwelling-room by a wall but as there was seldom a door attached to the opening between the room and the yard, the inmates of the yard, fowls, donkeys, dogs and even camels had access to the dwelling-room. The average family seemed to be the master, two or three wives and about six children, so the single room was rather a crowded affair. The odour from the village was definitely as the boys put it "on the nose" and we were amazed that anyone could live under these conditions and be more or less healthy. On the occasion of our visit to this village Horrie had been left behind at camp, but having his own idea about this, he emulated his escape in Crete and chewed through the string which he had been tied up with and followed us.

We were bargaining for a bottle of "very hygiene Cognac" when we heard the commotion. Arab villagers young and old flew up the narrow winding street accompanied by squawking fowls. The familiar bark of the wog-dog told us what was happening. Horrie had tracked us to the village and, apparently under the impression that he was going to rescue us, had launched a "blitz" on the village. He certainly did a good job. Up the street he came barking a clean sweep, behind him an empty street, before him everything the village boasted of including several donkeys who had taken alarm at the noise. Opposite to where we were standing, several Arabs had endeavoured to get through a small doorway together, and had become a yelling struggling mass of humanity. We called Horrie and tried to stop him, but by now he was thoroughly wrapped up in his work and no amount of calling made any difference. Thinking it might be a good idea if we made ourselves scarce, we ran through the street calling Horrie as we went. The wog-dog recognised another glorious evacuation and followed. I picked up the growling white pup and we broke our run down to a more dignified pace. We passed two fighting Arabs. Both had bleeding noses. Apparently one had rushed out of a doorway as the other rushed in, and each blamed the other. Their idea of fighting seemed to be to each grab a handful of the other's hair, kick with their bare but rough feet and yell. It was difficult preventing Horrie, from joining the free-for-all.

Once out of the village I put the wog-dog down again. He looked so pleased with himself that we could not help laughing. Horrie was not offended, but seemed to laugh also. He led the way back to camp, his little stub tail at right angle to the ruffled hair along his back.

We made it a rule to keep Horrie tied up during mess parades so that he would not cause disfavour by his presence in the cook-house. We used to bring scraps of cooked meat back to the tent for him after we had finished our meal. However, one morning we were surprised to find him eating and enjoying a piece of raw meat when we returned from breakfast. He was still tied up inside the tent and as none of the tent inmates had given him the meat, it was a mystery how he came by it. The same thing occurred again the following morning and the following. The next night Horrie was tied up and after our return from breakfast we noticed that the raw meat was missing. The mystery was solved during the day, the Battalion butcher arrived at the tent with Horrie's ration of meat. We learnt that the wog-dog had been visiting the butcher before we went to mess in the morning, he received his ration, returned with it to the tent, buried it in the sand within reach of the tent pole where we used to tie him, then while we were having our breakfast he uncovered his own at the approved breakfast time. Being tied up all night had prevented his early morning visit to the butcher who, missing the dog's visit, had brought the meat to the tent, and so solved Horrie's secret for us. From then until we left Palestine Horrie never failed to receive his ration of raw meat.

Leave to Jerusalem was granted so the Battalion and some of our platoon, including the wog-dog, set out to see the Holy City for the first time. The trip into Jerusalem was made in a wog bus and it was anything but boring. The Arab drivers of these buses put their lives and those of the occupants in the hands of Allah and let his head go. The tooting of anything behind was never taken as a signal that some vehicle wished to pass, but was accepted by the drivers as a challenge for a race. Of course the lads in the bus would invariably encourage the driver by saying "let her go, George," but George never needed much encouragement, and "let her go," he certainly would.

The road to Jerusalem was fairly good but narrow and the buses carry about thirty troops seated. Consequently there was little room to spare when two buses were abreast. However, the judgment of the Arab drivers was nothing short of amazing, and often there was little more than a coat of paint between two bus loads of pleasure-bent, cheering Aussie soldiers on leave.

Our first job in Jerusalem was to provide the wog-dog with a new harness and lead. We had a Greek two-drachma coin, a souvenir from Greece inscribed with his name, number and unit. "Horace, EX.I 2/1 M/G Bn." The EX.I inferring that Horrie was number one warrior from Egypt. The unit colour patch and the coin were attached to the harness which he proudly wore.

The sight of the little wog-dog being led, or rather leading us through the streets of Jerusalem caused quite an interest and it was not long before we were surrounded by numerous would-be guides. We selected a very bright Arab lad who assured us he was the son of Sandy McKenzie. After seeing such places as Bethlehem, The Garden of Gethsemane, we were guided to the Old City of Jerusalem. Horrie was left, much to his indignation, in the care of our guide "the son of Mr. McKenzie," while we went to see the inside of the Church of the

Holy Sepulchre. Although Horrie more or less accepted the attention of our Arab boy guide, he was anything but happy about being left with him, and he was very pleased when we returned.

The Wailing Wall of Jerusalem was next on the list. This old wall built by King Solomon in the year 1000 B.C. is one of the most holy of Jewish shrines and for generations Jews have been coming here making a pilgrimage to the wall. At night the rocks in this old wall are covered with dew, and legend declares that these are the tears shed by the rocks when weeping in unison with the Jews. Another legend declares that the old wall had been lost to sight by time and numerous battles in which the old city was destroyed. A reigning king had the wall uncovered by throwing a handful of coins over the earth that covered the wall and the Jews of Jerusalem uncovered the wall by scraping the earth away while searching for coins. Judging by the prices the Australian soldiers paid for articles in Jerusalem this legend is probably correct.

The Fast Hotel in Jerusalem had been taken over by the Australian Comforts Fund and had become the Australian Soldiers' Club. It was possible to get a bed and meals here for a very modest price, but there was no tariff for wog-dogs so Horrie was a non-paying guest for a few days' stay at the Fast Hotel.

Shortly after our return from Jerusalem we visited Gaza, a place well-known by many Diggers in the last war. Some of the buildings still showed signs of the shelling it received from Australian Artillery during the 1914-1918 war. Many of the boys uncovered pieces of shrapnel and shells on the old battlefields. About two miles out from the township of Gaza there was quite a good beach, and after a look around the town most of the Australian soldiers made their way there. The wog "wallads" (boys) were a nuisance here as it was impossible to leave clothing unattended on the beach. Horrie earned his rations by keeping guard over our clothing while we enjoyed a swim. He took his job very seriously and the "wallads" kept him busy. They would retire just out of reach in a circle and the wog-dog watching all sides at the one time, saw that they never got near enough to "klefty" (steal) anything. It was very hot work for the little pup and after we returned from the swim we would give the pup a cooler in the water and erect a shelter from the burning sun for him by sticking a few branches in the sand and covering them with shirts, etc. Horrie would enjoy his well-earned rest, but every now and again he would sit up and growl a warning to the "wallads" that he was still on the alert.

The ruins of the Ancient City of Ascalon were not far from our camp and we spent a little of our leisure hours on the beach at Ascalon and exploring these old ruins. Ascalon dates back to the days of the Saracens. The Crusaders fought many battles in and about Ascalon and it was during one of these battles that the city was destroyed about 1170 BC. There were apparently many splendid buildings erected here during the Roman rule, some relics had been collected and placed in a Roman bathing pool. King Herod the Great was born at Ascalon and during the Philistine times Ascalon was the centre of their culture and the stronghold of their hatred towards Israel. Many of the stone fragments bear Greek inscriptions and one stone bears the Greek legend "Forward Ascalon Forward Rome." Remains of a sea wall can still be seen on the beach, and pillars that had been sunk into the wall to help withstand the force of the sea have become exposed and point out to sea like defiant guns.

Horrie always accompanied us during our rambles. In fact he would look so dejected if we told him that he could not come that we usually took him in the end. He dearly loved these outings and was extremely interested in any new place, and of course there was always a rough chance of catching a lizard.

One night not very long after our arrival in Palestine, a lone enemy aircraft dropped a stick of three small bombs on our camp. Horrie, who was sleeping on the foot of my bed, was the first in our tent to hear the whine of the falling bombs. His barking woke us in time to hear the familiar whine and Horrie lead the scramble for the nearest slit trench. The bombs fell on clear ground and we were soon back again in bed. The little wog-dog was more annoyed than scared and at intervals during the remainder of the night I heard him growl.

As soon as it was daylight Horrie inspected the bomb craters and found there an Arab who also was interested in the craters. Horrie spotted him and I think blamed the Arab for disturbing his sleep during the night, because he growled his ultimatum to "imshee" (buzz off) or else. While the Arab was considering the ultimatum, Horrie, being a strong believer in taking the initiative, attacked with all his might. There being no time to "imshee" the Arab showed fight by picking up a stone. Of course a dog that has been through Greece and Crete cannot be frightened by a mere stone and the battle was brought to a satisfactory conclusion from the wog-dog's point of view by the flight of "George" and Horrie's return to us with a mouthful of wog pants.

During the day we dug several more slit trenches and as the area I was digging was close to our tent Horrie supervised and approved of the work. At midday Horrie was given an extra big bone as a reward for sounding the Air Raid alarm the previous night. The wog-dog thought it was a just reward and it was his treasured possession for many days. In fact he became so attached to it that he tried to take it to his and my bed with him. Fortunately it was too heavy for him to lift and although he tried to enlist my aid in this matter I failed to understand. So for safety he finally deposited it in the slit trench.

During the day Horrie as allowed to roam where he wished and he was often away on a ramble by himself for a whole day, but he would always return during the evening. One night he failed to return. We searched for him in some of the camps nearby but failed to find him. As he did not return the next day the search started in earnest. We visited every camp for miles around with his photograph, but although we got many clues, they all had the same result and Horrie remained among those missing. Eight days passed and we had almost given up hope of seeing the little wog-dog again. It seemed probable that he had been run over on the road where traffic passed to and fro in an almost endless stream during the day. We were sure he would have returned before this had not something happened to him.

On the ninth day after Horrie had disappeared some of the platoon went on leave to Tel Aviv. Included in the leave party was my friend Don Gill who was attached to Horrie as much as I was myself. In fact all the platoon and many others were attached to the little pup and Horrie would have had no trouble in finding an owner. After the leave party had been a few hours in Tel Aviv, they were making their way to a café when an excited bark attracted their attention. It was none other than the little wog-dog. He spotted them and came streaking across the road in and out of the traffic. The boys held their breath as Horrie dodged cars on the road, but he safely reached them and was beside himself with joy. He was much the worse for wear, covered with tar and oil and had lost a good bit of weight. In spite of all the oil and tar he was carried until they we were able to obtain a lead and collar for him. Taking Horrie to the café they tried to get him a feed, but the only thing in the way of meat that they could buy him was chicken sandwiches at 60 mils (1/6d.) a pop. Nothing but the best for the wog-dog who enjoyed the meat while the boys had the bread. After satisfying the wog-dog's appetite, the party adjourned to the Australian Soldiers Club where Horrie was treated to a pot of milk while the boys celebrated his return to the platoon.

Tel Aviv is a modern city. Thirty odd years ago this place was desolate sand dunes. With money supplied by the Jewish National Fund, the Jewish inhabitants of Jaffa built Tel Aviv which is the Jewish translation of "Altneuland." Jaffa itself is very old and is mentioned in ancient Egyptian history. The population of Jaffa is mostly Arabs, the Jewish inhabitants having moved to Tel Aviv. The fine beach at Tel Aviv has a holiday atmosphere about it. Brightly coloured beach chairs and tents dot the beach and on fine days there were always a good crowd of bathers. The wrecks of two ships somewhat spoil the scene. These two wrecks lay close in shore and the story that is told about them relates that they were filled with Jewish refugees from Europe who had sought to land at Tel Aviv. Being refused permission to land, the Captains of the ships ran their vessels ashore, thus compelling the authorities to permit the refugees to land.

The leave party eventually arrived back at camp plus Horrie who was given fourteen days C.B. for being A.W.L. He was so obviously pleased to be back again that it was impossible to scold him. We were never able to find out how he got to Tel Aviv which is some forty miles from where we were camped, but we came to the conclusion that he had boarded a leave bus in the camp and had alighted in Tel Aviv where he was lost until picked up by some of the boys.

We moved to several camps in Palestine and at one place named Khassa Horrie first became acquainted with "Imshee", an Arabic word meaning "buzz off" in Australian. Imshee was the same breed as Horrie and was the mascot of the 1st Australian Anti-Tank Regiment. She had also been in Greece, Crete and Syria. It was love at first sight and up till the time that the units became separated the two dogs were inseparable companions. If I wanted Horrie and he was not in Camp I could be sure of finding him at the other Reg. Often Horrie would bring his girl-friend home and share his meat with her. It was habit to chain Horrie up at night so that his attention to Imshee would not interfere with his night duty in guarding the rifles in the tent. Imshee would call for him first thing in the morning and away they would go on a lizard-hunting expedition for the day. The Anti-Tank Reg eventually left for Syria and Horrie lost his girl-friend for a while. He fretted a little and would often visit the site of the camp where Imshee had lived and it was while searching for his girl-friend that he became lost for the second time in Palestine.

This time Horrie was away five days and as luck would have it some of the boys found him on the road to Jerusalem some fifty miles from Khassa. The poor pup had undoubtedy travelled by foot and was very sore-footed when the boys picked him up. He was quite prepared to settle down again when they returned to camp but if the word "Imshee" was spoken he would become very excited.

About the end of November we were expecting a move to Syria, and as it was said to be very cold there we made Horrie a uniform. It was an elaborate affair made from a piece of old greatcoat. The edges were braided with white tape and the outfit was completed with brass buttons and a corporal's stripes.

While we were making the uniform Horrie stood quietly for some considerable time while we cut pieces here and there until it eventually fitted him. He was very proud and pleased with his uniform. As soon as it was fitted he did the rounds of the camp to show his many friends. The Corporal stripes were given to him so that he would be able to "stand-over" some of the other dogs that found the camp a good home.

The wog-dog's keen interest in everything often provided a laugh. One day when I was tuning in a wireless set Horrie parked himself near a pair of ear-phones. A voice speaking in Arabic from a local station came through fairly strong and the wog-dog heard the voice. He scouted around the tent but was unable to locate the Arab. He looked very questioningly at me then at the ear-phones, "there is something wrong here – an Arab in the camp that I cannot find." He sniffed the ear-phones, cocked his head on one side and then the other. Deciding that the ear-phones had something to do with it he growled and advanced in such a manner that I thought it wise to switch off the station.

Horrie was always prepared to his bit during a sing-song and the moment anyone started to play the mouth organ he would lift his head and sing as only a wog-dog can.

Whenever we went on leave the wog-dog accompanied us and he got to know the meaning of the word "leave." He would become very excited if the word was mentioned, and as he usually wore his uniform during these breaks from the monotony of camp life, we would tell him that he could go on leave if he knew where his uniform was. As I made a point of leaving it on a nail in the tent post, Horrie would jump up on the post and bark.

The wog-dog attracted much attention while wearing his uniform on leave, and very often civilians wished to pat him, but as he had spent almost all his short life among soldiers he was always mistrustful of anyone not wearing a uniform. Consequently the desire to pat him was cut short by a growl.

The Dead Sea, the Sea of Galilee, Haifa and many other places were visited by Horrie and he became well-known in Palestine.

About the beginning of December we moved up into Syria, and Horrie, as usual, displayed all interest in the trip by road. Damascus proved the first place of interest for us and the sight of a long avenue lined with gum trees brought back memories of home. The convoy stopped here for a few minutes and we alighted to enjoy the clean smell of the gums.

Damascus is believed by many to be the oldest settlement in the world. It is mentioned in the book of Genesis in the time of Abraham. It lies at the foot of Mount Iasyuan and along the bank of the river Barada and owing to this source of water there are many fine gardens and trees on the outskirts of the city. Damascus has a very mixed population, Moslems, Persians, Afgans, Kurds, Turk, Jews, Jebble Druze and French comprise most of the population and each year thousands of Moslims, of different races pass through on their pilgrimage to Mecca. As each wear their national costumes Damascus is probably the most colourful city of the east. Many names have been given to this city, some of which are Pearl of the. East, City of Many Pillars and Gate of Mecca. It took some little time to get used to the Syrian money as the Syrian pound note or one livre was worth approximately 2/10d Australian and after changing a Palestine one pound note for nine Syrian pound notes, we felt as though we were as Lord Haw Haw termed us "Menzies Millionaires."

From Damascus we continued north and up along the Lebanon valley until we reached the town of Ba'albek. The air now was very keen and snow could plainly be seen on top of the Lebanon mountains. There were some famous and interesting ruins at Ba'albek which first appear in history in the Hellenistic times as Heliopolis, the city of Heliopolitan Zeus. Ba'albeck became a Roman colony very early, probably under Augustus in 554. Much of the great temple was destroyed by lightning and fire. It was at this time the heart of Pagan worship. Three great temples formed the Acropolis of Ba'albek and the temple was turned into a fortress by the Moslems. Six huge columns of the temple of Jupiter still remain standing today and are an impressive land mark that towers above the old city of Ba'albek. As we continued up along the Lebanon valley the air became very cold and the little wog-dog lost some of his keen interest in the passing scenes.

Eventually we reached the small Lebanon city of Zaboude and this was to be our home for the following seven weeks. The snow season was fast approaching and much work was to be done to make ourselves comfortable for the winter. Huts known as Nissen huts were erected. These huts were built with a round roof so that the snow would slide off and so prevent any undue strain on the structure by the weight of snow on the roof. It was also necessary to anchor the huts down by passing strong wire over the roof and attaching it to iron pegs driven into the ground. This was done to prevent the huts from being blown away by a terrific wind that occasionally blew along the valley.

In spite of his warm uniform, Horrie took a very poor view of the cold and first thing each morning he found many starters for a game to warm up. It was entirely his own idea and he started it by taking a sock and scampering around with the boys chasing him. It was impossible to catch the elongated pup and we were always the first to become tired.

The natives from the nearby villages were very friendly and great gamblers. They often joined the boys in a game of two-up. Horrie immediately let them know how they stood with him and they avoided our particular hut like a plague.

After a few heavy showers of rain the camp area became very muddy and it was necessary to provide the wog-dog with a kennel as he got far too muddy to sleep in his usual place on the foot of my bed.

Not long after our arrival in Zaboude, Horrie became sick and very sorry for himself. The sudden change to cold weather was a little too much for the wog-dog and he caught what appeared to be the 'flu. We wrapped him up well and kept him warm with rocks that we heated in a fire, then putting them into his bed. A special diet of warm porridge and milk was provided for him and there were so many callers to our hut to inquire after him that for two days we issued a bulletin on his condition and posted it on the outside of the hut door.

Horrie was very sick for five days but he made a rapid recovery when a visitor by the name of "Imshee" was brought to see him by some lads from the 1st Anti-Tank Regiment who had arrived and camped alongside us. The arrival of his girl-friend Imshee who also proudly displayed a uniform, made us wonder if the wog-dog had been malingering as his recovery on seeing her again was certainly rapid. But perhaps his pride in being an old canine warrior prevented him from appearing sickly while the worshiping Imshee was about.

A few days after Horrie's recovery, Don Gill and I took Horrie on a hunting trip into the Lebanon mountains, where Cheetah, Gazelle, Fox and Wolf were supposed to be numerous, according to the local natives. Just exactly what part Horrie was going to play during the hunt, we were not sure, but he was ready to tackle all-comers. The little wog-dog's eagerness to get into the hunt got us into a spot of bother very early in the piece as he rounded up some Evacualand natives who were digging a tank trap. These cheerful Africans treated Horrie as a joke but the pup was fair-dinkum and did not realise that they were wearing our guernsey.

There was panic among these chaps when the first fall of snow occured some little time later. Being from the heart of Africa they were not familiar with snow and when the flakes began to fall they donned their gas-masks thinking it was a gas attack.

Shortly after passing the tank trap we came upon a Vichy French tank of ancient vintage. Of course Horrie had to investigate it and he scrambled in and looked out the observation hatch with an expression that meant trouble for the enemy. There being no enemy visible Horrie expressed his satisfaction with the situation.

After climbing for some time we encountered two Syrian sheperds. They were greatly taken with the little wog-dog and wanted to pet him, but it was only with protest that Horrie allowed them to pick him up. As all the dogs in the Lebanon mountains show sign of the wolf strain, a small pup like Horrie, especially wearing a uniform, was a novel sight for these sheperds.

At about half-way up the mountain we passed through a small village and obtained the help of a small boy as guide for the remainder of the journey. The village itself was similar in most respects to the village in Palestine except that they were much cleaner. Each house boasted of one room containing a fireplace in one corner and several recesses in the walls in which bedding was stored during the day. At night the floor was covered with soft eiderdowns and cushions and the inmates removed their footwear and slept on the floor in their clothes.

Outside the home of our guide, corn had been spread out on square pieces of cloth in the sun to dry, while a watchful eye was kept on the fowls by a member of the family.

Leaving the village behind we continued up along a deep gorge. The mountain was very rocky and covered with bush that resembled holly. These bushes grow to about five feet in height and seemed to be the main diet of the mountain goats that roamed the hills and valleys under the care of small boy shepherd. Although our guide said "Plenty gazelle" it seemed as though we would return empty handed. However, a deep-throated growl brought us to a sudden stop and there, only a few yards before us, stood the nearest approach to a cross between a wolf and a lion I have ever seen with or without the aid of rum with a H (A Syrian rum that many Aussies will remember). This huge wild mountain dog must have been fascinated by Horrie as it completely ignored us but stood facing Horrie who in turn was as game as only a little wog-dog could be. He advanced in front of us with tail as erect as a mast, full of fight and obviously intent upon protecting us. Don covered the beast with his rifle while I commanded Horrie to stand fast. I managed to snap the two dogs facing each other, then made a grab at Horrie with the intention of picking him up but Horrie perhaps sensing my intention or mistaking it for an advance, sailed straight into attack followed by Don, the Syrian boy guide and myself. The sudden mass attack was too much for the wolf-dog and he promptly beat a hasty retreat with Horrie right on his heels. Although we called to Horrie, he was determined to follow up the retreat and there was nothing else for it but for us to follow. Down the mountain side we raced after the two dogs, gaining terrific speed, dodging boulders and bushes and yelling to Horrie to stop. But Horrie managed to secure a toe hold and the Syrian dog stopped and in turn got a hold on Horrie's neck and shook him like a rat. Just at this moment we arrived at the spot with no hope of pulling up in a perpendicular position, and stacks on the mill was the order of the day. Fortunately for Horrie the big dog let go and scampered off and this time the little wog-dog was securely held and prevented from following. A shot in the air was sufficient to convince the big fellah that absence of body is better than presence of mind, and the last we saw of him was his huge body disappearing behind some bushes further on down the valley.

Horrie took a particularly lean view of not being able to follow and the growling, bristling pup had to be carried for some considerable time to prevent him from taking pursuit.

Our Syrian guide informed us that it was his own dog. This completely dispelled our idea that Horrie was a wolf-hunter although the wog-dog continued to growl for the remainder of the day to remind us that we were perfectly safe with his protection.

After some two hours climbing we reached the top and were rewarded with a magnificent view of the Lebanon valley far below, where, from time to time throughout the ages, the noise of battle and marching feet of soldiers of many nations has echoed. As dusk was approaching we made our weary way back to our guide's home where we were to stay for the night. On reaching the home we removed our boots and were made comfortable near the small fire in the one room that comprised the whole dwelling. The little wog-dog was not at all happy about our hosts. He kept very close to me and greeted the attention that the Syrian family paid him with poor grace.

Tea was served soon after our arrival and as there was some eight people in the room and only one small table standing some twelve inches high and measuring about eight inches in diameter, tea was a sort of two at a time arrangement starting with us and finishing up with the two female occupants. The food consisted of olives, cheese and brown bread shaped like a pancake and not all agreeable to our palates. Following the golden rule "When in Rome do as the Romans" we consumed our "Mungaree" (food) under the watchful and approving eyes of the whole "flamin'" family. Our gallant effort was rewarded with smiles and another helping even larger than the first.

When at last the meal was over, cushions and eiderdowns were spread over the floor and we were soon asleep. Horrie took up his usual position at my feet and I doubt if he slept at all as several times during the night he growled at any movement on the part of our Syrian hosts.

Early next morning we started out for camp and to please our guide I took his photo standing on the roof of his home and holding the unwilling Horrie.

On our return to camp we learned of the Japs' attack on Pearl Harbour. There was much speculation as to what the future would hold for us, and almost everyone expected our return home to face the new enemy that now threatened Australia.

Christmas Day arrived and with it the first fall of snow. The inevitable snow-man soon appeared and Horrie and Imshee scampered through the snow, much to their delight. Actually Horrie was too under-slung for the snow country and his method of travelling was by leaps and bounds. Often two eyes and a little black nose was all one could see of the wog-dog.

After the thaw set in the nights became bitterly cold and as a foot-warmer Horrie excelled himself, to such an extent that he had an open invitation from all the occupants of our hut to sleep on the foot of their bed. Horrie had his own idea about keeping warm, and although his box under my bed was scarcely large enough he managed to squeeze Imshee in with him.

The hard icy surface soon affected Horrie's feet and although we endeavoured to keep his pads soft by smearing them with vaseline it became necessary to provide him with a sledge to enable him to accompany us on various outings. There was always many lads prepared to take a turn hauling the sledge and the wog-dog in turn did much in his own little way to repay this luxurious method of travelling.

As the icy surface upon the roads made travelling treacherous for rubber-tyred vehicles. The ice had to be chipped on dangerous sections of the road and when we were employed on this task we always took the wog-dog with us and he was given the job of guarding our clothes. Another job that Horrie was called upon to perform was to pass a telephone line through a culvert under a road. This was managed by attaching the telephone line to Horrie's collar and someone would hold him at the entrance to the culvert on one side of the road while I called him from the other. He soon realised what he was required to do and he performed this service for us on many occasions.

The second fall of snow was reputed to be the heaviest for twenty years and the section of the valley where we camped received some fall of eighteen inches. Many passes in the hills were completely blocked and traffic was at a standstill for a few days. Although the mantle of white made the nearby village, the valley and the mountains a beautiful sight, the novelty soon wore thin and we were wishing for the warmth of the sunny south.

It was not long before we were to get our wish as the usual signs of a move became apparent, and on the 26th January we started on the first leg of our journey. There was much speculation on our ultimate destination, Australia being a very strong favourite. Java and the Western Desert were next with New Guinea as a rough outsider.

Very soon old familiar sights appeared and to welcome us back Palestine had taken a beautiful coat of green. As we now firmly believed that we were to return to Australia we were impatient for the next move. The tragic bewildering news of the fall of Singapore and the loss of our 8th Divy. made matters a hundred percent worse, and the troops were anxious and irritable as the long days passed. At about this time a problem had to be faced - Horrie, and we hardly dared think of it. Everyone was particularly tender to the little pup who received this added attention with some concern. On numerous occasions he would look up into my face with such a searching expression that I know he realised that his fate was entirely in our hands.

Was this stout-hearted, gallant and faithful little friend to be destroyed, or worse, left behind to fend for himself once again in the friendless desert? "What are you going to do with Horrie?" This question was asked by the little wog-dog's numerous friends. "I don't know yet," was all I could reply, but the fact remained that something had to be done, and done quickly.

I have endeavoured through the last pages you have read to try and convey just what a large part this little chap played in our lines as soldiers on foreign soil. Because a soldier is trained to kill, wound and maim the enemy he is more or less at times reduced to the primitive state of man, the inevitable reaction often presents itself in a longing to show affection. Apart from the Australians natural love of animals I think this may have been the reason why Horrie received such a lot of kind-hearted attention from his many friends. You have probably guessed that an earnest effort to reward the little dog's untiring faithfulness was to be made, and what could be more suitable than a good home in the best place we knew for him to spend the remainder of his days. Our first step was to take Horrie into Tel Aviv for a close examination. It was necessary to leave Horrie for seven days and when we returned for him his joy at being with us again is more than I can describe. As we imagined, Horrie was in perfect condition and free from any disease whatsoever, so one worry was eliminated. Horrie was provided with a new harness on a lead and treated to a glass of milk and a feed at the Australian Soldiers Club in Tel Aviv before we returned to camp. Expecting that anything could happen Horrie was never let out of sight for the next few days. Even at night if we went to a picture show which was close by, Horrie went also and many soldiers will remember him there. He displayed keen interest in the pictures and by standing on my lap and putting his two front paws on the back rest of the seat in front he could see what was going on - often growling at dogs and cattle that appeared on the screen.

At last the order came that all pets were to be destroyed. We had been expecting this order and the necessary provisions for Horrie's disappearance had been completed. Firstly it was given out that rather than destroy Horrie we would give him to a Palestine Police Station not far distant from where we were camped, and this was actually done with much fuss and "to do".

The remainder of this narrative will surprise many soldiers, who still think that Horrie is a mascot of the Palestine Police. I contacted an English Policeman and told him something of the little dog's adventures, explaining that we were unable to take him home with us. Naturally he was very pleased to accept Horrie as a gift and the little wog-dog was left in good hands. As we walked away we could hear the little dog barking in an effort to make us understand that he did not want to be left behind, but we had to stick to our carefully prepared plan and we returned to the camp without him. Everyone in our section looked as though he had lost a very good friend and although a few knew of the plan they kept quiet. Many were not at all happy about leaving Horrie and suggested that at least I might have made an effort to get him home, but we considered that to make more certain that our plan would go smoothly it was necessary to let everyone believe that at last Horrie was no longer part of the unit and with the exception of a few this was rigidly adhered to. Two important jobs had to be done that night. One was to get Horrie back into camp unobserved and the other to provide a hiding place for him in camp. This was very successfully done by digging a hole in the sandy floor of our tent and under my bed. The hole was sunk down to a depth of five feet and measuring some five feet long by two feet wide. The sand that was removed from the hole had to be taken out of the tent unobserved. This was managed with a bucket and proved rather a long job. However, when we considered the hole large enough three bearers were placed over the hole and a cane mat that I used for a mattress was rolled over the hole. We were very pleased with the result as it was very unlikely that anyone could guess that the mattress concealed such an effective hiding place. The job was finished off by putting some old clothes in one corner for a bed and a drinking dish in the other. This was to be Horrie's hiding place during the day. There was just sufficient space between the splicing of the mattress to enable Horrie to get a little air.

The next job was to get the little wog-dog back again. This proved quite simple as I returned to the Police Station that night and whistled. Not very long after I heard a yelp of delight and down the pathway alongside the building came the little pup. I do not know just how he got out, but he managed his part of the plan all right, and very soon we were swallowed up in the darkness. I got back to the tent without anyone seeing the dog. I carried him under my arm and wrapped in a towel. Once inside the tent we had great difficulty in keeping Horrie quiet as he made such a fuss about being home again with his old friends. When he had quietened down a little we tried him in his hiding place and he quickly realised that he was to remain there without making any noise. At first he was inclined to think this was a new game but we impressed upon him that this was definitely necessary as only one bark or yelp would have been fatal. During the whole of the daylight hours for nine days Horrie remained silent in his hiding place and as there was a tent inspection every day, we often ceased to breathe for a few minutes. As soon as it was dark we took him out of the hole and after concealing him under the arm, walked some distance from the camp and there let him get some exercise under cover of darkness.

The next problem was his transport during the eventual move. This proved fairly difficult as on previous occasions a blind eye was very helpful. But this, the most important move of all, had to be managed without even any suspicion of Horrie being among us.

Most of Horrie's previous moves had been accomplished in a sea-kit bag so that method had to be ruled out as too conspicuous. There seemed only one method left, that being in a pack. Each night during Horrie's exercise I trained him to sit in the pack and not move. Poor Horrie! These days were not the best for him, but he was quite happy and accepted the strange things as being all in the game. The length of time he spent in the pack varied from at first five minutes until two hours at the end of his training and although he must have been anything but comfortable, he did not so much as move. After being allowed out of the pack I made a great fuss of him and in the end I had only to put the pack on the ground and he would try to get into it without my help.

After Horrie's training and exercise at night, he was allowed to spend the remainder of the night on the foot of my bed, but as soon as daylight arrived, back he went again into the hole under my bed.

At last came the great test, as it had been decided to practice a move out of camp and a short march with all our gear. It almost proved fatal for Horrie. All his previous training in the pack had been done in the cool of the night, but during the trial the day proved very hot and poor Horrie must have endured the tortures of the damned in the hot pack. However, in spite of this he only moved once and after being told to keep still he did not move again. The test was quite successful as no one suspected Horrie's presence, but it was apparent that some big improvement was necessary in the pack. After a few experiments a fairly comfortable arrangement was made with the pack.

We made a light frame from plywood to fit inside the pack, the top piece of plywood being hinged so that Horrie could be put inside. The light frame kept the pack square and prevented the sides from folding in on him. This gave the little pup more room, in fact he could sit upright without any trouble. The back portion of the pack, which, when in carrying position rested against the carrier's back, was cut to enable Horrie to get more air. The hole in the back of the pack was criss-crossed with string to keep him in. Horrie was very pleased with this improved method and seemed fairly comfortable.

Eventually the day of the move arrived but with it another problem. We were to move during the night, but during the day the tents had to be taken down and the area cleaned up. This, of course, meant that the cane mattress had to be removed out of sight. Fortunately not far from the camp there was a small wooden building used as a Canteen. After explaining to the Sergeant in Charge that it was necessary to keep Horrie out of sight during the day, he readily agreed to keep the wog-dog out of sight for us in one corner of the shed, so just before daylight, Horrie was removed from his old hiding place and so kept out of sight until it was possible to pick him up again during the following night.

All went well and we moved during the early hours of the morning to the point of embarkation on the Palestine railroad. Luck was with us as Don and I were able to get into the guard's van and so let Horrie out during the journey the Egyptian border. A few hundred mils squared the Guard, and we reached the border without any mishap. We alighted at a spot on the border and Horrie was once more put out of sight inside the pack. We had a meal at this place but when the pack containing the wog-dog was placed on the ground it had to be placed upright so as to enable Horrie to remain in a sitting position. Naturally the back of the pack had to be covered up and during this procedure, Horrie was spotted by one of our Officers. A smile and the thumbs-up sign indicated that all was not lost.

The remainder of the journey to the port from where we were to embark was completed without mishap, but Horrie was compelled to do the journey in the pack. We arrived at the transit camp not far from the port and once again we were fortunate in being able to get a tent for ourselves. That night Horrie was able to get a little exercise some short distance from the camp. The next day we formed up again for the march to the ship. As it was particularly hot, Don carried the pack containing Horrie and I marched behind so as to be able to talk to Horrie and encourage him and if necessary cover up any movement he might make. During the march to the embarkation point, the heat was terrific and I could hear Horrie panting inside the pack, but not a sign of a move did he make. He was panting so hard that in an effort to relieve him a little I wet my fingers from my water bottle and poked them into the pack at the top to enable him to lick them. What the poor little chap endured during that march was typical of his stout little heart.

We arrived at the wharf without mishap, and while the boys were picking up their sea-kit bags I was able to take the pack from Don's back and stand it on the wharf so that a slight breeze blew into it from the hole in the back. I spoke to Horrie and could hear his little stub tail brushing along the bottom of the pack. He was still game and confident we were doing our best for him.

Now came the big test. Would there be a kit inspection? Fortunataly there was not and we were ferried out to an American ship that was to bring us safely home to Australia.

Once on board half the battle had been won, but even then if Horrie had been discovered it would have been the finish for the little wog-dog. After his confidence in us we were not going to relax our effort. We were in luck as we were allotted to a cabin complete with a shower room and we so wangled it that all in the cabin were cobbers of Horrie.

Once settled in the cabin, Horrie was allowed out of the pack, but not before the door had been snibbed and locked. We gave the wog-dog a cool bath and a drink. The poor little chap was about all in and after placing him on a bunk under the air inlet, he soon slept the deep sleep of an exhausted pup.

That night we got under way, all tired but happy in the thought we were returning home. Horrie occupied the best spot in the cabin, that being on the foot of a bunk directly under the inlet that supplied the cabin with fresh air. Absolutely no risks were taken during the trip home. Horrie did not see daylight again until we landed. Each morning, during cabin inspection, Horrie was put back into the pack and the pack was neatly stacked with the rest of my equipment on the head of the bunk and all went well. During the day we took it in turns to stay below with him. The cabin door was always locked and would be opened only in answer to a special event of a strange knock, Horrie was put back into the pack and stacked away. The inmate of the cabin would then open the door and act as though he had just awakened from a sleep to explain the delay in opening the door.

Crossing the line, the heat below deck was very oppressive and we took it in turns to wet Horrie and fan him with a towel. Often when asleep Horrie would whimper, probably dreaming of the trials he endured in our effort to allow him to spend the reminder of his days in a well-deserved good home.

The trip home was uneventful and glorious days of sunshine were enjoyed by the troops who spent most of their time in the good old Australian game of two-up. The Yanks joined in and everywhere was the feeling of good fellowship among the American sailors and Aussie soldiers.

We longed to let Horrie scamper about the deck, but did not chance anything going wrong, so the little wog-dog had to remain below. As long as he had company he did not seem to mind, and after all it was a slight improvement on his previous existence in holes dug in the ground and packs.

The day of days arrived and at last out of the haze the dim outline of Aussie appeared. Cheer after cheer arose from the ship. We were home again.

Horrie left the ship in the same manner that he boarded it, but there were still a few obstacles to overcome. The first was to plant him safely until we had been assured that he would be quarantined and not merely destroyed as was the reward of Imshee's faithfulness. We were fortunate.

Horrie was well cared for by good friends and until we were able to have him quarantined, his presence was a closely guarded secret.

Our ambition was realised and the little wog-dog won through.

What less could we do for such a stout-hearted faithful little companion.

After some eighteen months service with the A.I.F., the little wog-dog has been honourably discharged and today he enjoys he comfort and happiness of a well-cared for suburban dog. He has grown fat in his new found home and spends many hours lazing and sleeping in the sun, and who knows, perhaps he dreams of his eventful days in the Army, of the heat and dust of the friendless Egyptian Desert and the elusive lizards: Perhaps of Greece, Crete, bombs and shipwrecks, or maybe the snow of the Lebanon mountains or the wogs of Palestine or perhaps Imshee.

63 Questions

ION IDRIESS

QUESTIONS

A. Please describe, in all detail that you remember, the dog when he first joined up. Colour, size, anything at all about him. And, as he later developed, any particular characteristics whatever. As described now, he is but a "shadow dog". Hence, it is very necessary that any habit, any peculiarity, any characteristics should be described, both on adoption and as he grew, so that a picture of a "live" dog can be quickly built up in the readers mind.

I understand that the dog may be in Sydney. If so, I'd like the address and a chance to go out and see him.

Also, re photos. Any photos of him, together with interesting photos of the Battalions adventures would help the book immensely. P.S, Mr Cousins has since told me he already has the photos.

B. Who is Big Jim Hewitt? He is only mentioned in the very last line, yet apparently he had quite a lot to do with the dog.

As you read the questions you will repeatedly see "give names of cobbers, scraps of conversation etc" This will all help to build up the book. Not only the dog, but the men closely associated with him must be "living characters" for the book to live.

1. Was it on an expedition to the old Roman city that you found Horrie? What were the names of your companions? Do remember any scraps of conversation re the dog? For instance, who suggested name of Wog-Dog? Any particular reason for the name Horrie?

2. Dog covered his feed with sand. Who said "you can scarcely blame him"? (names and scraps of conversation always make an incident more interesting). Who was the spark suggested he might be an Italian dog?

3. Who were your tent mates who took most interest in the dog?

4. While on route marches, the Arab urchins back chat, especially in regard to the dog would win a laugh from the reader. Slip in as many witty remarks or incidents, occurring at any time, or on any occasion, as you can possibly remember.

5. When about to move from Egypt the question was "What about Horrie?" Please think up a few scraps of conversation, any suggestions the boys made i.e. It will make the story more personal and convincing. Give names whenever you remember. Also any little details in training Horrie to the kit bag.

6. Any amusing incidents during the train trip?

7. One of the boys called "Yow", to what does this refer?

8. Re ships crew and their dog. A few personal incidents about members of the crew, their dog, and still more of Horrie, aboard ship would add to interest.

9. The sea sickness incident is quite good. Any more cheery little touches would be appreciated by the reader anyway.

10. When you made a life jacket for Horrie, what were names of cobbers who lent a hand, or took an interest? Throughout the entire book please add these little details, they will add a much more personal and sympathetic touch to the whole story.

11. Horrie and the stork at Larassa is quite good. Any similar incidents, anything about the dog and the Greek kids, any little touch that brings in the dog and the local inhabitants, or picturesque localities, or customs, will add to interest.

12. Re Mt. Olympus, Servia Pass etc. Could you give a very short pen picture of these and any other outstanding local positions mentioned throughout the M.S. The reader will be keenly interested in any "local touch" relating to any part of, or life of, Greece.

13. Description of dog detecting planes, good. Also sensitiveness. This could be enlarged on throughout the M.S. by relating any particular incidents which would be a highlight of such characteristics.

14. Remember "those who knew him well" etc. Always give names of the. boys who were "closest" to the dog. Hence, the reader will get to "know the whole crowd."

15. The retreat is good, could be made better by further incidents here and there. Such a touch as the Greek folk filling in bomb craters so that the convoys could proceed without delay, will show the reader the spirit of the Greek folk. Do you remember any other vivid incidents of the retreat?

16. What name your troopship? Do you remember names of any escorting ships?

17. On Crete. You left Horrie with the boys for· awhile. What names?

18. The adoption of Henriette not quite clear. What was the soldier's name who thought she was Horrie? What troopship or crew did she belong to, etc.

19. Please give descriptions of Henriette. Any characteristics.

20. "We searched all night for the wog-dog", who is we?

21. Describe just a little of your job on Crete.

22. Name of ship in which you evacuated from Crete.

23. "Dier Suneia was rather interesting during the first few weeks of our stay there." Why?

24. When you had a look around the village near Dier Suneia, who were your cobbers? Do you remember any scraps of conversation?

25. A few more little pen pictures of Jerusalem would be appreciated by readers.

26. The story of Horrie guarding the clothes against the Wallads while you bathed is good. Throughout the M.S. any similar little incidents whatever will all help to build up the dogs character - and the book.

27. The little description of Ascalon is O.K. Don't forget similar touches where opportunity occurs, and bring Horrie in whenever possible, also scraps of conversation from your mates.

28. Please give all details you can of Imshee – and her reputation. This is a bit of good stuff. Don't forget any incident in which the lady features.

29. When making the uniform - do you remember any conversation? and who were the principals etc?

30. The incident with the Arab through the earphones is good. Do you remember any others similar? Or any joke re the sing songs. The dog knowing when he was going on leave too, is good. Any such the little characteristics are well worth the telling.

31 The Dead-Sea, Haifa, etc. he became well known in Palestine. How? Please give any details you can remember.

32. A few details of natives joining in a game of two-up would be interesting. Did they know the game beforehand? Were they sports? etc. etc.

33. Re Bulletin as to Horrie's condition when he became sick. What would be the wording etc?

34. Imshee arrives. If you could give a few details of the meeting it would make humorous reading. Get the old memory to work for you as much as you can about Horrie and Imshee.

35. Describe a little more clearly these "cheery Africans who treated Horrie as a joke". Also give details of the incident when snow fell and the Africans donned gas masks. It should make an interesting page or two.

36. Just a few little details of Lebanon Mts., their inhabitants, and the dog life there, would be quite interesting. Any little "local colour" at all that you've forgotten to mention.

37. The description of the Wog-dog-and chase is quite good. If you remember any more details, send them along.

38. You snapped the two dogs. If you have any interesting photos at all, send them along. They will help a great deal.

39. When the boys heard of the attack on Pearl Harbour, do you remember any scraps of conversation that expressed their sentiments? Such would be very interesting.

40. Don' t forget to bring in Imshee wherever possible.

41. The sledge. "The wog-dog much his own little way to repay this luxurious method of travelling." A few little incidents illustrating how, would bring the reader closer in touch with the dog.

42. The dog pulls telephone line through culvert. Anywhere in the M.S. whenever the dog helps in a job of any sort, please mention it.

43. Australia, Java, Western Desert, New Guinea. Please give scraps of conversation as the boys speculated on this move. It brings in the "personal touch".

44. What did boys say and think about fall of Singapore and loss of 8th Division?

45. "The dog knew something was doing, etc". If you could enlarge on this, the boys' concern, and the dog knowing there was something in the wind, it would help the story quite a lot. Don't forget your cobbers names in any questions or conversations re the dog and your probable plans etc.

46. "Took Horrie into Tel Aviv for a close examination" Please explain what for; the reasons etc., if there was any other reason apart from health of dog.

47. If you could enlarge a little on Horrie at the picture show it would add to the interest and humour.

48. The scheme is complete. But I think that here you had better let me into this. Describe the conversation and men among whom the scheme was finalised. It may be better to let the reader into the secret at this stage. Describe difficulties that you know beforehand you will be up against.

49. Any of the lads who actually practically helped in the scheme, should be mentioned as the scheme develops.

50. Please give a little conversation where lads not in the know suggested you should at least try to get Horrie home etc.

51. All details would now very much interest the reader. For instance, just how did you get the sand unobserved from the tent, etc. Please give all details of the whole job.

52. Don't forget names of your tent mates, and all who were particularly interested in the dog, all these men should be familiar to the reader by now. For instance, what was conversation when you got dog back into tent, and were questioning him, and teaching him he had to remain quiet, etc.

53. It might be a good idea to give a short description of a tent inspection with Horrie in hiding.

54. Horrie must be transported in a pack. Could you give details of the dark scheme, when it was being planned, conversation etc. Also, some little description of the training.

55. "It was necessary to explain to the sergeant in charge that it was necessary to keep Horrie out of sight etc." Who was this friendly sergeant? Bring him in to the story eariier, if he "fits in". Also, remember conversation with him etc.

56. "Horrie was spotted by one of our officers". Please describe folk who were there, and this incident in detail.

57. What port did you embark at, some further little detail of the march would go well.

58. "So wangled it that all in the cabin were cobbers of Horrie," If you could remember details and conversation of how this was planned, it would add to the interest.

59. A little about the sport of the troops; going home, would brighten the story.

60. Description of looking after Horrie in the cabin is good, but could be enlarged to advantage. Don't forget names of your mates, and any interesting scraps of conversation. And how about cabin inspection?

61. Imshee is mentioned. Was she on the same ship?

62. How did you plan about the quarantine, etc.

63. Could you give a few details of Horrie's present whereabouts.

*The advent of 'Horrie' the little wog dog, he is having a
bath a few days before we left Egypt for Greece.*

*Some of the Signallers and Horrie, all wearing the caps that I
received in Kay Kruger's parcel.*

(Top) June 1941, Palestine; Bill Graham, Alan Hitch, Horrie and myself; (Lower) Horrie and Wilberforce the pet rabbit, up to the time of writing Horrie has shown admirable restraint.

*December 1941. I wonder if one could see a sight like this in
any army but the Australian. 'I doubt it.'*

Don Gill and Horrie taken outside the home of a Jebble Druz in the mountains, these people are excellent fighters and fortunately friendly to the British.

Horrie faces one of the huge mountain dogs, just after this snap was taken I picked him up and he was very offended as he wanted to start a blue. I doubt if there ever was a little dog as game as he is, you will see by the snap he certainly has his tail up.

(Top) Horrie receives his Christmas dinner; (Lower) Jerry visits our camp in Palestine, bomb craters near our tent.

(Top) Horrie in Damascus; (Lower) Some of the boys having a game with Horrie. We were always the first to get tired.

(Top) Our camp at Zaboude in the Lebanon valley, the round roofs were known as Nissan huts. Or snow roofs; (Lower) Horrie and I on top of the mountain, you can see the Lebanon valley far below, during the climb we often had to rest about every twenty yards as the going was so steep.

Dec.24th I managed to get away for two days leave and together with another chap spent the two days in the mountains, this time however we hired a Jebble Druz guide and donkey. This snap was taken while we were having a bite to eat. 'Antoine' the guides name was our 'very good friend.'

Antoine's son and Horrie taken on the roof of the house. We stayed the night here and slept in the one room, about twelve in all. These people simply spread mats on the floor, remove their footwear and lay down to sleep. Horrie during the night must have remained awake as several times he growled when anyone moved in their sleep, he just does not trust wogs, although we were in perfectly good company.

Naturally Horrie wanted to be in on the fun and in this snap you will see him in a world of whiteness. Owing to him being so under slung the going was very heavy but in spite of his little legs he enjoyed himself immensely. I used to vaseline his pads each night to prevent them cracking. This snap was taken in the valley where we had a fall of 18 inches.

(Top) Taken at the scene of an accident, it was a beauty, four trucks being involved but they all kept on their wheels, neither the wog dog nor myself were hurt; (Lower) Horrie even objects to the wog removing rubbish from outside our tent.

Jan. 30th 1942, my birthday and George McMillan popped up. He is camped only a few hundred yards away, we arranged a football match between the two units; good game and good beer.

Taken at the Australia Club in Tel Aviv, good Aussie beer but Horrie preferred milk. Left to right; Don Gill, Horrie and Clarrie.

*(Top) Horrie guarding the camp; (Lower) Horrie, the civilian, taken
in Melbourne, three years to the month after we first found him.
Horrie is unable to soldier on now, being too plump for his uniform
and pack.*

The Story of Corporal Horrie

The Signal Platoon of the 2/1ˢᵗ Machine Gun Battalion were those most interested in Horrie. He was generally accepted by the platoon as their mascot, however as he spent all his time in my particular section I will try and describe the various members of this section who really had the most interest in Horrie.

Our particular section was known as the Rebel section, probably because its various members were in trouble of some little kind. If the cookhouse was raided during the night, the Rebels got the blame. Anyone sporting a shiner (black eye) after a days leave, it probably was a member of the Rebels. The parade state each morning (the Sergeants report of the members of this particular section on parade and duty etc) On parade 10, duties 5, sick 2, AWL 2, mostly those among the missing were from the rebel section, however in spite of their ability to get into trouble they were a pretty good crew and quite capable of doing a good job when necessary.

George Murchison, (a NSW lad) known to the Rebels as Murchie. In civilian life a Car Salesman among almost every other job you could name. Age about 25, height 5'10" sturdy and very agile, grey eyes and a perpetual grin, he was our Sig. Officers no.1. problem-child.

It was impossible for him to keep out of mischief, an absolute menace with fire-arms, our tent roof was full of holes through Murchie's indiscriminate firing, purely accidental as he would put it, his sandy hair would never be brushed, boots never cleaned if he could possibly help it and a habit of not standing very close to his razor when shaving, as long as he scraped the soap off he considered it good enough. However his ability as a Signaller was excellent, which helped the Sig. Officer to overlook some of Murchie's shortcomings. He would spend about 10 mins on his early morning toilet and about anything between one and a half hours on his rifle, he was easily the best shot in our section also.

Next to his rifle or lethal weapon as he termed it, his hobby, much to our discomfort was catching snakes and keeping them in a kerosene tin under his bed. At the most unexpected moment he would produce an

Asp (small Egyptian snake about 12" to 18" long) from his pocket, this unholy habit often caused trouble.

I recall one incident in Alexandria when the Rebels were on leave, having selected a Café where we could have a drink in comfort, I handed my hat to the waiter at his request to hang it up. Murchie said "Hang this up with it" 'this' was an 'asp' he had produced from his pocket. The waiter, badly scared, backed onto the table behind him completely upsetting the glasses of beer upon it, I saw the occupants who happened to be Tommy soldiers. Of course they didn't like it and in spite of our offer to pay for the spilt beer a blue (brawl) started. Tommies joined Tommies and Aussies joined Aussies. The call of 'Coppers' united the Tommies and Aussies and we evacuated, the only capture 'I hope' was Murchie's 'asp'. "Not a bad start," declared Murchie,"We've only been in Alex 20 minutes!"

Sorry to relate Murchie is now somewhere in Java, but we can quite imagine him running his own little war back up in the hills somewhere, and who knows perhaps we might meet up with him again one of these days. This incident happened before the advent of Horrie.

George Harlor, (NSW also) known as Gordie about 30 years of age, very dark complexion and hair, Wireless Mechanic in civil life, brown eyes, rather quiet disposition on the surface, lean and about 5' 8" high. Gordie was a wizard with wireless which helped our section very considerably, a few scraps of odds and ends and a wire or two and Gordie had a wireless.

His ability eventually got him into a wireless section of the army much to our sorrow and Gordie's also, but he is in his right job now and after all there is a war on. As the Arabs called everyone George we renamed our dark cobber Gordie at his own request.

Bert Fitzsimmons, known as Fitz to the Rebels, tall, a shade under 6ft, quick wit, lean build, a very close cobber of Gordie's, also possessed laughing blue eyes. In civilian life a Farmer, Fitz also came from

NSW. Age about 27 years. If Fitz was ever required in his leisure hours one could always find him running a 'two up' game.

I recall an incident typical of Fitz, a blitz was declared on two-up games in the camp lines, Fitz reorganised the game into marbles, the game being played as near as possible to the officers mess. Fitz's pet word was 'finish' he got this word from the Arabs who use it extensively. Should you ask an Arab shopkeeper for an article which he has not got, he merely says 'finish' its expressive and final. After we returned to Australia Fitz got himself married to a very nice Sydney lass 'Finish Fitz' he is still with the unit, but in another company. A wife and now a little daughter, also keeps Fitz out of trouble these days.

Brian Featherstone, Feathers to the Rebels. Feathers was the baby of the rebel section, age 21 years, about 5'8", sturdy build, blue eyes, sandy hair and a very fresh boyish complexion.(Shipping Clerk in civil life) Feathers was the direct opposite to Murchie in appearance. Extremely smart in attire as far as possible in the A.I.F. turn out, also smart in drill movements. Feathers hailed from Melbourne. He was an excellent Signaller and his ability at signalling earned him one stripe, which his high boyish spirits made the holding of same, rather uncertain. Feathers was always ready for a spot of fun and he was still able to blush in spite of two years overseas service with the A.I.F.

Bill Thegog, known as the Gogg to us. The Gogg hailed from South Australia, he rejoiced in some 26 years. Medium coloured hair, rather shallow complexion, about 5' 9"in height, a quick wit and a hard doer. In civilian life, a Barley Inspector. The Gogg was a very capable sort of a cove, good signaller, excellent sportsman and an artist with a pencil or brush. Also an artist with the booze if any obtainable. The Gogg brightened up the Rebels tent with numerous drawings of dusky damsels.

Don Gill, known as plain Don to the Rebels, hailed from NSW, very dark hair, brown eyes, about 25 years old, rather quiet, an excellent cobber, stick like chewing gum to a blanket, and my own particular side kick (cobber) Don like myself was attached to the Signal platoon as Don R's (Dispatch Riders).

Roy Brooker, the Signal Sergeant, known as Poppa to the Rebels. We were very lucky here in having a real gem, Poppa must have been a bit careless when giving his age on joining. Fifty winters and as many summers would be near the truth. Hair not too plentiful, mousy grey, light blue eyes, height about 5' 8" solid frame. In civic life, a Railway Clerk and hailed from Geelong, Vic.

Service with the 1st A.I.F at Gallipoli and the desert had not cured his appetite for adventure, neither had it slowed him up any, he often set a pace that made the younger chaps sit up. Luckily the rebel section was the pride of his life although he made a point of telling us different.

A real fair dinkum Aussie, Poppa, heart like a lion, and he possessed that rare knack of understanding human individual complexes and so able to get the best out of anyone willingly. Poppa saw the distance out with us over there, but on return to Australia he was dropped back to B Class on account of his age. We were a miserable mob the day he left us and that day marked the end of his beloved rebel section, after Poppa left us 'she came unstuck'.

Lt. Jim Hewitt, Big Jim to the Rebels, here again we were fortunate in having a good man. To measure up to Big Jim you need to be about 6'3" shoulders like a working bullock, a capacity for work that makes a draught horse look like a sissy, extra keen sense of duty that often secretly clashed with a sense of humour. Age about 28 years, blue eyes, hailed from Warracknabeal, Vic.

Excellent sportsman and particularly keen in anything he tackled. We got along pretty well with Big Jim and no doubt gave him a few extra worries just for good measure, however he had our complete confidence and we would back him to the last. Big Jim shared in our love for little Horrie and his blind eye was a great help on many occasions. Unfortunately we were to lose him also on our return as he was transferred to another unit. All the Rebels including Poppa tried to get a transfer with him but we were unsuccessful.

Don and myself were the first to find Horrie and it came about in the following manner. Our jobs in the platoon were motor cycle dispatch riders, when not actually employed on a dispatch run we spent the days in maintenance and repairs to the cycles, after tinkering about with the engines we would often give the cycle a try out across the rocky and sandy desert that made up the Ikingi Maruit area. Ikingi Maruit was on the fringe of the Western Desert and some twenty odd miles from Alex.

As the going was fairly rough for cycles we knocked out a fair bit of them and acquired a little experience in rough riding that later stood us in very good stead. We evolved a little game to make these trips across the sandy waste more interesting, the idea being to ride on a compass bearing for a certain distance, then another bearing was taken until a trip of five or six legs of various bearings was completed. We started the first leg from a point known as the Wogs Bakehouse, it was a rough shed arrangement where the bread (and sand) was baked for the troops by Arabs under the supervision of Tommy soldiers.

Before starting we agreed upon a bearing and distance for the first leg, then one rider would away about half an hour before the following rider. After completing the leg the first rider would then select another bearing and distance and write it down on a piece of paper, place it on the ground and cover it with a small heap of stones, making the heap about twelve inches high, he would then complete the second leg and repeat the procedure until five or six legs were completed. The task of the following rider was to complete the first leg, locate the heap of stones and so get the clue for the second leg. It was fairly difficult as one had to ride exactly on the bearing otherwise difficulty was experienced in finding the small mound of stones, to keep on the bearing all sorts of obstacles were encountered such as deep shifting sands, and in parts rocky surfaces, these spots had to be negotiated without deviating far from the bearing.

On this particular day I was first away and having completed the last leg was waiting for Don to catch up. Propping the cycle up I sat in the small shade it offered and dreamingly smoked a cigarette. My attention was attracted to a tiny white object darting across my line of sight. Coming to life I stood up and watched a small pup racing from rock to rock. He did not appear to notice my presence as his entire interest was in his task of trying to catch small lizards that darted from rock to rock in order to escape him. Amused I stood quietly watching him when the noise of Don's approaching cycle attracted his attention. His alert little ears were pricked to catch the sound and he watched Don approach me with an enquiring look. As Don stopped and dismounted the pup withdrew a little distance and continued to cautiously watch us. I drew Don's attention to the pup and remarked "I wonder what that little bloke is doing way out here?" The last leg had taken us well out into the sandy waste, there being nothing but sand and rock for some fifteen odd miles in circumference. "Looks like he's blown through from somewhere," I answered. ('blown through' is a term used by the troops meaning absent without leave) "He's a funny looking little joker," exclaimed Don.

The little pup by this time had decided we were not as important as the lizards and had resumed his self-appointed task of ridding the Egyptian desert of lizards. He certainly was a funny looking little joker, he was all white except for a broad sandy coloured stripe along his back, he stood about twelve inches high on very short little legs, the front two legs were similar in shape to that of a bull dog, the length of his body was all out of proportion to his height. In fact 'Longfellow' was suggested as a name for him by Feathers, his sharp little ears alternately stood to attention and stood easy and he possessed a tiny little stub tail that stood as erect as a mast.

He was a bit doubtful about us at first and our efforts to get him to come to us were unsuccessful, as we called him he would view us with his little head on one side then turn his attention once again to the lizards. "Do you reckon he's an Arab dog?" "Could be anything

I guess," replied Don, "He certainly doesn't seem to understand our lingo." 'Here pup', 'Good dog', 'Here boy', etc meant nothing to the little pup, although when we called him he would watch us cautiously, he did not seem exactly afraid.

Eventually we won his confidence by turning rocks over and sending the lizards that hid underneath scurrying in all directions. The pups little stub tail betrayed a good view of our effort to help him, he would select one particular lizard, however the chosen one would invariably escape him and seek shelter under another rock. The little pup would look up at us with his beautiful brown eyes appealing to us for further assistance. 'This is not a game, I'm hungry' they seemed to say. I eventually picked him up and I could feel his little ribs only just covered by his silky soft short haired coat.

"Doesn't seem to be doing so good," I remarked. Don patted his head "Poor little pup, only a puppy too." We guessed his age to be about six months. "We might feed him up a bit back at camp," I suggested. "Good idea," replied Don.

By this time the pup had gained complete confidence, and resting his chin on my arm he closed his eyes. The problem was then to get him back to camp but we managed this by leaving my motorcycle behind and I rode behind Don holding the pup in my arms. Although the trip back to camp was fairly rough the pup did not seem at all worried, in fact he seemed quite contented. Later that day Don and I doubled back to retrieve the cycle.

It was just before midday when we hit the camp and all the Rebels had returned for the midday meal from various jobs, when we entered the tent they were all bashing the spine. "What the hell have you got there?" exclaimed the Gogg, noticing the pup under my arm. "Our new mascot," replied Don. The Rebels all got up and came over to my bed where Don and I had sat down, we told them how we happened to find him and they all agreed the pup could do with a good square meal. Fitz first noticed the pup was sporting a few fleas and exclaimed "He's a bit lousy," Murchie piped up with "Well you're a bit crummy (lousy) yourself." "All dogs have fleas," quoted Gordie scratching himself unconsciously. The call of mess parade headquarters from the orderly NCO was the signal for dinner, so we tied the pup to the tent pole and wandered across to mess.

Each of the Rebels returned with a portion of meat for the pup. An old plate was produced from somewhere and a huge feed was placed on the ground within reach of the pup, we retired to our various beds to watch the result.

The pup cautiously sniffed here and there around the plate, then promptly started shovelling sand over the plate, using his nose as a shovel, every now and again he would stop, sniff again, then recommence until he was satisfied that no smell escaped from the little mound. "Wouldn't that rip yer!" from Murchie. Gordie said you could scarcely blame him. Fitz reckoned that the meal was on the bugle (nose) alright. The Gogg enquired, "Do you think he may be an Iti dog (Italian) and require olive oil with his food?" As the pup was obviously hungry we reckoned it was worthwhile giving the oil a try.

I elected to scrounge a little oil from the R.A.P while Don removed the plate of sand covered meat and washed the sand from it. Lightly covering the meat with olive oil we again offered it to the pup, strange as it seems it was exactly what he required, and to the accompaniment of much tail wagging, he wolfed down the scraps of meat. "How did you work that one out Gogg?" inquired Don. "Just fluked it," replied the Gogg. "Righto you blokes on your feet!" greeted us as Poppa came into the tent.

"Hello what's going on now?" as he spotted the pup. "Don't go near him," from Murchie in a serious tone. Poppa stopped and inquired "Why?" "We don't want you passing fleas over to our little dog," Murchie replied. Poppa remarked that the little pup must be well and truly contaminated by now, as nothing could remain unaffected in the midst of so many nit-wits. Poppa however took to the pup right from the start. "What do you say we keep him for a mascot," I inquired, Poppa and the rest of the Rebels thought it a good idea.

"Murchie's snakes will have to go though," suggested Feathers. Surprisingly to us Murchie agreed. "There's no flaming kick in them anyway," he declared. Fitz then related how during the morning Murchie brought forth his box of tricks and endeavoured to put a little life into the sluggish snakes. Connecting a lead from one terminal of a car battery to his tin of tricks and holding the other lead from the battery, he would touch the snake inducing sparks to pass between the snake and the tin, the result was electrifying to say the least.

Murchie a little reluctantly disposed of his pet asps under the strict supervision of all the Rebels. "You know Cleopatra died by clutching an asp to her breast after learning Mark Antony had been killed," he told us, previous to this we had accepted his word that asps were really harmless. "Murchie will be the cause of white flowers under someone's photo one of these days," declared Poppa, "and if you ever bring another pet snake within my sight it'll be your own photo."

"Well I guess we had better give the little pup a bath," I suggested. Don got a tin and some water from the cookhouse while I scrounged through Feathers gear for his life-buoy soap, the rest of the Rebels disappeared as Poppa mentioned something about a working party for a job. The little pup looked very miserable while we washed him, he cer-tainly had his full quota of fleas, however he accepted the bath in good grace. After the wash we dried him on Fitz's towel, when the toilet was completed the pup was as pleased as punch, he scampered in and out of the tent and up and down upon the beds, making himself thoroughly at home. "Looks like he will stay" remarked Don as we stood watching the happy pup, there was little doubt about it that the pup was prepared to accept our offer to join the 2nd Ack. for better or worse.

Later that afternoon when the rest of the Rebels drifted back, the pup, bright and shiny as a new pin, greeted each as they came into the tent with a wag of approval. Shortly before tea Big Jim popped in and seeing the pup picked the willing little chap up and patted him. "What name this fella George?" he inquired immediately setting us another problem.

Feathers suggested Longfella, this described the pup alright but the Gogg pointed out that you cannot walk about calling out Longfella, Longfella, if you required the pup, as the rest of the mob would think you were 'desert happy.' Gordie said don't call him George or we will have half the wogs in Egypt answering the call.

Don suggested we call him Roy after our good friend Poppa, but Murchie reckoned it wasn't a fair go for the pup as he looked far too intelligent to be called after Poppa. However Big Jim remarked that as we already had one mascot called 'Erb' why not call the pup 'Orrie.' 'Erb and Orrie' usually go together.

We debated this title and eventually agreed to give the pup the full title 'Horace' however as time went on the name developed into Horrie, probably because it was easier to call 'Horrie' than 'Horace'.

The question of breed came up also that night. Murchie suggested he might be a cross between an 'Upsetter' and a 'Disappointer'. The Gogg said that as the olive oil strongly suggested some breed of Italian dog he may be an 'Iti-dale'. Gordie declared that he was probably some breed of Arab dog who had once been owned by an Italian, perhaps an Arab terrier. Fitz immediately popped up with 'Arab dog.' 'Wog dog,' this name caught on all over the camp, if anyone spoke to the dog it was either 'Horrie' or 'Wog dog', but if talking about him it was 'Horrie the Wog Dog'.

Horrie showed an intense interest in everything, often when the Rebels were discussing various matters I would catch Horrie watching their faces closely and listening to every word. He also showed a very marked dislike for the natives, he not only adopted the manner of a watch dog, but he actually hated them. He was also very fond of riding on trucks, any of the Rebels only had to open a truck door and Horrie would scramble in, he was quite friendly with all the lads in the unit but he showed a very marked liking for the rebel section, we were undoubtedly his favourite cobbers.

Parades and route marches were his very special joy particularly route marches, if a platoon should march by our tent he would join them and bark his invitation to us to join in also, however finding that he was unable to persuade us to join in, he would come trotting back without any of us calling him. "Next time Horrie," I often told him and he would wag his tail, quite content to stay with us, although he would watch the disappearing platoon until out of sight.

When our platoon was out on a route march, Horrie would take up position at the head of the column, tail erect, head held high and ears cocked, he was as proud as punch, obviously impressed with his own importance; often he would look back at us for approval, we always managed to occupy the front ranks and so be able to keep an eye on him, as the numerous trucks that passed along the road, were always a danger. Horrie after a very short period became very obedient and he would instantly obey any of the Rebels.

'Come alongside,' was enough to bring him close to my heels. I trained him to obey this command by first attaching a long length of fishing line to his collar, giving him the full length of line I would call "Come alongside" at the same time gently but firmly drawing him towards me until he came to heel. He was surprisingly quick to learn anything that was required of him, and Poppa often declared he was by far the most intelligent member of the rebel section and certainly the most obedient.

Big Jim had us out on a route march one day and as we approached a small native village he gave the order to march to attention; usually after clearing the camp area we were 'marched at ease' this meaning that one could carry the rifle in the slung position, it being far more comfortable, also one could talk, whistle or sing which helped the miles to tag past, apparently it was his idea to put on a bit of a show for the natives benefit.

At the order we straightened up, checked the slopes of the rifles, heads up, chins in, chest out, belly in etc and stacked it on in general. Dozens of Arab urchins flocked from the village dwellings to see such a splendid sight, however the show came unstuck as one little urchin called in a tiny voice 'march at ease' the splendid sight collapsed amid much laughter from the boys. Murchie fell victim to the wit of one small urchin one day much to our delight; "Saieda George" (good day) exclaimed Murchie to the little urchin. The urchin noticed Murchie's disreputable appearance and returned the greeting with "Good morning wog."

Saieda was very commonly used by the troops but after this particular incident very few were game to say Saieda to Murchie for quite awhile. No matter how friendly we were to these little urchins, Horrie would never accept them in anything but poor grace, it was only the command to 'stand fast' that prevented him from setting the urchins on their way. Many of them were likable chaps and full of cunning to extract a little 'Baksheesh' (give me something) from the troops. Often one would say quietly 'Baksheesh Sergeant' knowing all the time a man was only a Private. This effort was accepted in good humour by the troops and the cunning urchin usually received a few 'mils'.

A parade of any description was the signal for Horrie to become very excited, this intense excitement of Horrie's often expressed itself as only a dog may, but however there are very few trees in the desert and in some places few rocks also. This particular incident happened during a Battalion parade.

Our company was formed up in platoons for a preliminary inspection before moving off to the Battalion parade ground. Feathers this day happened to have charge of the Signal platoon and looking spick and span as usual, stood out from the rest of us like an organ stop. Horrie scampered around for sheer joy and his excitement was beyond control when another Company passed us on their way to the Battalion parade ground. Just at this moment Big Jim advanced towards the platoon. Feathers sprang to attention and stood like a statue, prepared to hand over the platoon to Big Jim. Horrie in his intense excitement mistook Feather's boot for a rock, the incident may have passed without the platoon bursting but unfortunately a stray dog that had been following the Company that had just passed us noted Horrie's mistake and pre-pared to do likewise.

The mob absolutely burst. Feathers who was unconscious of the comedy was taken by surprise at the wealth of mirth from the ranks, he turned about sharply and ordered quiet everywhere "Firm as a rock." Fitz quickly replied "That's what Horrie thought." The mob just buckled up, it took ten minutes to quieten them and seven days CB to forget the incident. Feathers when let into the joke later took it in good form and Horrie only wagged his tail in reply to Feather's scolding.

Often during the day Horrie, noting that nothing much was doing in our direction, would wander through the camp, visiting his many friends in various tents. However one particular day he returned to us limping. We examined the hind leg that seemed to worry him but were unable to find anything wrong. Later that day we were informed that Horrie had shot out of one particular tent with a yelp, the only occupant in the tent at the time was a particularly nasty type of individual who unfortunately was able, and did, hide behind three stripes, it was also well known in the unit that he detested dogs.

We were pretty sure Horrie's friendly visit was greeted with a boot. After being informed of the incident Murchie was all for doing so and so over right away, but we talked him into better reasoning. "This needs careful handling" I advised, "As actually Horrie has no right to be in the camp at all", we therefore could not complain to those in authority.

Also no matter what the cause of ill feeling might be, a bit expensive to 'do a Sergeant over'. However it was not very long after that the account was squared up to our satisfaction.

This particular individual happened to be the Sergeant of the Guard one night not long after the incident. Part of his duty as Sergeant of the Guard was to visit each post to see that everything was in order. While on his tour of inspection he was halted in the dark by a muffled voice, "Halt, who goes there?" He halted and replied "Sergeant of the Squad." "Sergeant so and so?" enquired the muffled voice. "Yes," he replied. "Well... " said the muffled voice, "Cop this!"

He sported a beautiful 'shiner' in the morning. A check-up was made but at the time of the incident all the Rebels were in their tent. Poppa the Signal Sergeant was there to prove it. Horrie proved there had been no mistake on his part as he would always growl when he sighted the insect. Horrie did not forget and neither did the insect.

When the rumour first went around about the move from Egypt, Big Jim was away from the unit attending a Signal School, also absent was the Gogg, who had got himself mixed up in an argument with a Garry while on leave in Alexandria. (A Garry is a horse drawn vehicle something like a cross between a Hansom Cab and a Jinker) The Gogg got the worst of the argument and the result was a spell in hospital, we did not see the Gogg again until our return from Crete.

During the absence of Big Jim, Poppa ran the show, and his enthusiasm about checking over and adjusting our signal gear gave us an idea that something was in the wind.

The Rebels put all they had into getting the signal gear ship-shape and at the same time trying to draw Poppa out as to what was doing, Poppa was almost breaking his neck to tell us, but apart from saying that we might move we could get nothing definite out of him.

Don suggested that we were returning home so that Poppa could lead the Anzac march through Melbourne. Fitz reckoned that Poppa was too old to see the distance of the march out. Gordie reckoned that the rebel section could carry him, just like they were carrying him now. But all the bickering just passed over Poppa's head or beneath his feet and no answer was the stern reply to our efforts to get him to tell us where we were likely to go.

Don and I were issued with two new motor cycles and our days were busy running in the new engines and checking and adjusting etc. Giving the cycles a try out one day we dropped into Alex as I wanted to try and get some spools for my camera. They were very hard to get in those days as the troops had bought up almost all the available stock. After trying several shops we entered one that was owned by a Greek, he spoke quite good English and in answer to my inquiry for spools he replied, "Sorry boys I have none, but you will be able to buy plenty in Greece." We made no reply to this tempting statement and thanking him we returned to where we had left the cycles. "Looks like we will have to manage with the few spools we have got," I remarked to Don. "Seems like it," he replied. "I wonder what the Greek knows?" asked Don. I was wondering the same thing.

That night in our tent we talked the incident over with the Rebels. Gordie remarked "That's the shot sure enough, Greece." We were inclined to agree with him as the weight of our gear had been assessed and the boxes etc had been measured in cubic feet, this pointed to a move where shipping space was to be reckoned with. Poppa entered during the discussion and picking Horrie up sat down on the edge of my bed. "Poor little wog dog," he remarked patting Horrie, "We'll be sorry to lose you." "If we go anywhere, Horrie goes also," replied Feathers. Poppa grinned, "I was just wondering if you were slipping that's all," he answered. "Listen you prehistoric worm," declared Murchie, "the only thing likely to slip around here is my fist." Poppa laughed, "Relax," he replied, "You will get all the scrapping you want before very long." "So the move is definitely on?" I enquired. "Certainly is," replied Poppa.

Murchie asked Poppa if he was going to remain behind and look after the kit bags. "You will take your own kit bags and I will take you," replied Poppa. "Here is the news but keep it under your hat," continued Poppa "First of all mail closes tomorrow at 1700 hrs. (5pm) so if you have any letters to post, get them to the orderly room before 5 o'clock. The transport is going ahead the following day and I suggest that there might be room with the gear for something about the size of the little wog dog. Don and Jim will probably take their motorcycles and travel with the Transport platoon."

This seemed a good chance of getting Horrie away with us, as we could probably conceal him in the back of one of the trucks, and as Don and I would be with the Transport we could keep an eye on Horrie. "I'll pop over to the Transport tent and chat to Ron Ford," I suggested.

Ron Ford was a cobber of ours and was one of the drivers, leaving the Rebels talking I strode across the camp to Ron Fords tent. The Transport platoon were flat out writing letters. "Fordy about?" I enquired. "He's down at the truck lines," replied Reg Jenks, another of the drivers. "Did you get the drill?" (news) he asked me. "Yes," I replied, "I believe you pull out the day after tomorrow." Reg agreed and stated that he thought we would be going to Greece. "That's the Rebel's idea also," I replied.

Locating Ron Ford in the truck lines, I asked him if he could put Horrie in with the gear in his truck for the approaching trip. "Certainly," he replied. "Horrie can travel in the cabin of the truck and I will fix the window so he cannot be seen." We arranged little details about a tin for water to be in the cabin of the truck so Horrie may drink, also sufficient meat for two days to be placed in the cabin just in case Ron was unable to get to the truck once it had been put on the ship. "Don and I will probably be travelling with you also," I mentioned, "And between us we should be able to watch where the truck is loaded on board the ship and keep an eye on Horrie."

I returned to the Rebels tent and informed them of the scheme, they thought it okay. The Rebels remained up until late that night busy writing letters home, probably this might be the last chance of writing home for a fair while.

The following morning Don and I were informed that we were to load the motorcycles into the back of one of the trucks and that we were to travel with the Signal Platoon and not the Transport platoon.

The more I thought of it the less I liked the idea of Horrie being separated from us and I told the Rebels of the fact, thinking it over they agreed; no doubt Ron Ford would do all in his power to help the little dog but what if anything happened to the ship and Horrie was trapped in the cabin of a truck and Ron was unable to reach the truck to give the pup a chance.

We decided against Horrie going with the Transport. "Let's get our heads together and work out some other scheme," I asked them. "Once we get Horrie on board he should be alright," suggested Don.

Fitz was not so sure. "There are probably some fairly strict quarantine regulations that would prove a snag and the ships crew might put Horrie's 'weights up'." "Horrie is quite alright, Murchie should be the one to be quarantined if anyone," declared Feathers. Don remarked, "One thing, Horrie is only a little joker, there should not be much trouble, in fact he would put into a sea-kit bag quite easily" (A sea-kit bag accompanies the soldier when he is travelling on water, it contains a change of clothes, toilet gear and a few personal belongings, normally the larger universal kit-bag is stowed away on ship and not seen again until the destination is reached.)

"We might manage to get him on the ship unobserved if he will keep quiet in a sea-kit bag," I replied, "But we could hardly keep him in the bag for two or three days, don't forget he has his arrangements to make also." "I think I have the right answer to that problem," declared Feathers. "About two days travelling from Alex to Greece would be about the length of the trip, agree?" "Yes, that should be fairly near the mark." "Well then, counting Poppa there are six of us in all; divide six into forty eight hours and we have eight hours each." "Feathers has been well-educated," observed Fitz. "He went through college on a bike" declared Murchie. "Never mind them Feathers, continue with the scheme," I laughed.

"Once on board we will find a latrine and let Horrie out of the bag, we could each take it in turns to stop in the latrine for eight hours each, providing we had a book to read the time would pass quickly enough, of course we could relieve each other for meals," and, continued Feathers, getting his own back:

"I'll save Murchie the trouble on his shift and take his meals to him!" Murchie replied, "Another crack like that Feathers and you'll be lucky if you even see the ship." "Seems a good idea," I remarked "But I see two snags; one, Horrie may violently reject being confined in a sea-kit bag, and the second may be to find a single seater on the ship, you know the arrangements they usually have for troops, we will have to trust to luck about the single seater, but we could give the sea-kit bag a try out. Where is Horrie?" I asked. "Poppa has him sitting up on the sig. gear to keep the wogs away," replied Gordie. "I'll go and get him," volunteered Murchie. "Better speak to him as you approach," advised Feathers, "Or else he may mistake you for a wog in the dark." "I'll attend to you later... " drifted into us as Murchie strode over to where the signal gear was packed. Shortly afterwards, Horrie and Murchie appeared accompanied by Poppa.

"Fitz, you go over and take Horrie's place for awhile," ordered Poppa. "Ok," replied Fitz, "It would be a poor show if anything was pinched at this stage of the game."

"Well, what's the new idea?" asked Poppa.

We outlined the scheme to him and he approved of it, adding a good suggestion to improve on it.

"Get hold of a piece of cardboard and print 'Out of Order' on it," he advised, "We can tack it up on the door of the latrine, this should prevent the inmate and Horrie from visitors." Poppa also added that he was willing to do his shift of eight hours.

Murchie replied that if the latrine had 'Gentlemen' written up over the door, Poppa could ignore it and do his shift just the same. Gordie produced a sea-kit bag and Don picked Horrie up and lowered him stern first into the bag while I held it.

Horrie kicked a bit when his two little hind legs were first thrust into the bag, however I lowered the bag to the floor and once his feet touched something firm he stopped kicking. We inserted poor Horrie in up to his neck, but it then became obvious that it was not practicable to carry the bag by the string running through the top of the bag, as Horrie's supply of air would be cut off. We cut a hole in the side of the bag near the top and eventually got his little head out through the hole. The bag could then be carried by the string without choking the pup.

With the exception of Horrie we were quite pleased with the result, but it looked so comical that we all laughed. Poor Horrie, after he was let out of the bag he made his way to my bed and settling down he rested his chin on his leg and looked very miserable. I picked him up, "I think the little bloke is offended because we laughed at him," I remarked.

Horrie very quickly received plenty of attention: 'Poor little wog dog.' 'He's a good pup.' 'Pretty smart dog our Horrie,' and a few more reassuring words from the boys soon got the little stub tail wagging again and a happy expression on his face.

Plenty of praise and patting accompanied his next try out which he accepted as all in the game, it could not be said he actually liked it but he was not offended.

A choice bone was given to him after the second trial, and we considered that number one problem was solved, that being the method of getting him onto the ship unobserved.

The next we were busy putting the final touches to the packing of signal gear etc, following this, our own personal gear was packed, the contents of my sea-kit bag being split up among the Rebels in order that Horrie could be carried in it.

Long after lights out that night I lay awake unable to sleep, Horrie seemed restless also and he crept from the foot of my bed and finally rested his little chin on my arm. I lay thinking for a long time what the future had in store for us and many other things including quite a lot of home and Aussie.

A match flaring up to light a cigarette told me Don was unable to sleep also "What's up Dig?" I enquired, "Not sleepy?" "No," replied Don. "I was wondering if that last letter I wrote will get home safely." "I should think so," I replied. "Funny you know," he continued, "Little things you would like to say in a letter home, seem sort of sissy when you write them down." "Yes, I know," I replied, "Reckon she will be pretty willing in Greece." "Yes I think so too." "Wonder how Poppa will go?" "He'll be Jake I think," I replied. "Sorry the Gogg and Big Jim are not with us." "Yes," I replied, "Me too." "What about putting a brew on you blokes!" came from Murchie's direction. "Can't you sleep either?" enquired Don. "No," said Murchie, "I can't remember which box I put the Bren magazines in that I loaded with armour piercing." "No sugar in my tea…" came from the direction of Fitz's bed, "And none for me either!" called Gordie.

Don and I got the primus going and we were all soon sitting around it waiting for the Billy to boil. Poppa came in while we were pouring it out, "Heard the voices," he explained, "Not mine," replied Feathers from his corner, "I was waiting for them to wake me up and offer a mug of tea." "You lazy so and so," replied Murchie. "Our last night in the land of milk and honey," said Poppa. 'Bring your own bees and cows," replied Fitz.

The train journey from Ikingi Maruit to the wharf at Alexandria was accomplished in record time as it took only two and a half hours to travel some sixteen odd miles. During one of the numerous stops along the route, Arab urchins and adult vendors walked up and down along the train calling to the troops who were all looking and hanging out of the windows and doors: "Eggs is cook." " Eggs on bread," cried the hopefuls, offering boiled but dirty looking eggs and rolls of bread. "Scotch whiskey George," offered one wog to Murchie who was causing numerous fights among the Arab urchins by throwing coins into the crowd. "Good whiskey!" said the wog casting a half cunning look around him. "Shufti George," (show me) replied Murchie.

The wog casting looks about him moved nearer to the carriage window and handed the bottle to Murchie. Murchie examined the label and the cork closely, undoubtedly Scotch and the seal is unbroken he told us. Murchie paid 500mils (12/-) for the bottle. "Cheap," he remarked, fondly handling the bottle while we watched the wog disappear into the crowd. "Open it up Murchie," advised Poppa. Murchie opened it up and offered me the first drink.

A wink from Poppa advised me to say "After you Dig." Murchie took a good deep gulp followed by a mad scramble for the window, his cheeks bulging amid roars of laughter from the mob. "Cold weak tea," Poppa informed us with the smug knowing look of an old desert campaigner, fortunately for the wogs we were under way again.

Closely examining the bottle we found a fine round mark on the bottom of the bottle, in some manner a round piece of glass had been removed from the bottom, the contents drained and replaced with weak tea and the piece put back in. "He should not be allowed out by himself," declared Poppa. "Well…" sighed Murchie, "That was the 500 mils I owed you."

The ships crew were all members of the R.N. The ship was named the *Chakla,* 3100 tons, she had made numerous crossings between Alexandria and Greece carrying Aussie soldiers. Our particular passage near Greece was called Bomb Alley and the crew prior to our trip had always been met by a welcoming party of Jerry planes, probably operating from the Dodecanese islands. The crew were very interested in Horrie as their own little dog was very similar.

Extra good blokes voted by all the Aussie soldiers. When the rough weather got most of the boys on their backs the crew had hot tea always available for the sickly ones. One sailor asked me if he could show Horrie to the old man. Murchie overhearing him asked if he meant Poppa, however Horrie was displayed before the Captain. Poppa disappeared for awhile and later appeared with a piece of fat he had got from the ship's cook. Sitting down alongside Murchie he commenced to eat it, making a ghastly sucking sound at the same time. Murchie turned to me, "You couldn't beat that old B- with a stick in each hand." Poppa laughed, "Don't worry Murchie, she won't sink." "That's what's worrying me," replied Murchie with a groan.

We are getting near Bomb Alley one sailor informed us. Murchie, Fitz, Gordie and Feathers were not much interested in Bomb Alley or any other alley at the time. However Don and I were feeling a little better, Horrie had recovered quite a bit also.

We had been instructed to make sure we wore life jackets at all times, noticing that Fitz had discarded his, I advised "Better put your life jacket on Fitz." "Give mine to Horrie," replied Fitz. "Do you think a pup could swim in a sea like this?" I asked Poppa. "Not for long I should say," he replied. "Couldn't we fit Horrie up with a life jacket?" asked Don,"It might help a bit anyway if anything happened."

The idea appealed. I remembered a torn life jacket that had been discarded and I wandered off to get it. The jacket comprised of slabs of cork sown inside canvas to form a vest, the pieces of cork were about 8 inches long by 4 inches wide and about 1 inch thick.

We selected three pieces of cork in fair condition and cut them from the jacket making a kind of saddle, one strip each side and one on the back. I called Horrie who was playing with Ben and we fitted the saddle over him. I received a very inquiring look from the wog dog, but after talking to him he was satisfied that all was in order. Ben stood off a good safe distance and watched Horrie with interest. Horrie in turn wagged his tail and hindquarters making our job to fit him more difficult. Don hacked a half moon out of one end of the centre piece of the cork and so enabled the jacket to be pulled well forward, the idea being to keep the head more buoyant than the stern end.

The problem was then to fasten the jacket in place, the suggestion of string was discarded as it would cut into his belly, however a 2 inch bandage supplied by one of the sailors was the ideal thing. After winding the entire length of the bandage around Horrie's middle the jacket was held securely in place.

Very pleased, we surveyed probably the first dog's life jacket. "Off you go!" from me was sufficient for Horrie to join Ben. Ben sniffed and looked inquiringly at the life jacket, Horrie, who had forgotten the life jacket for a moment in his impatience to join Ben, suddenly remembered it, he rolled over on his back and kicked his little legs, this being of no avail to remove the thing he scrambled to his feet and gave a fair imitation of a 'Willi Willi'. Ben barked his encouragement accompanied by a few sickly laughs from the troops.

Horrie again unsuccessful stopped and invited Ben to give a hand. Ben fastened his teeth on the bandage and bracing his legs tugged so hard that he pulled Horrie on top of him. When they had sorted themselves out the bandage had become unfastened, Ben quickly seized the dangling end of the bandage. I called Horrie with the intention of removing the unwanted life jacket. Horrie started to move over to me but Ben held on to the bandage.

Horrie quite forgetting that Ben was only trying to help him turned on Ben and growled. The little wog dog came trotting over to me and while I was removing the jacket Horrie barked back to Ben that 'he won't be long.' Ben still cautiously watched him from a safe distance.

Our Transport platoon arrived in Greece before the actual declaration of war between Greece and Germany, a train service was still in operation between Athens and Berlin. Athens contained a fair sprinkling of Nazis who passed under the disguise of tourists, in many cases the Nazi insignia was openly worn on arm bands.

After the arrival of the Australian troops the insignia was often replaced with black eyes and thick lips, but as no state of war existed then between the Greeks and the Germans the so called German tourists had as much right to be in Greece as we did and the Australians had to stop this form of sport as it was not likely to improve the already rather strained relations between Greece and Germany.

We who arrived after the actual declaration of war were not fortunate to get leave to Athens as we started our long trip north almost immediately after our arrival in Greece.

As our convoy of trucks laden with soldiers passed through the outskirts of Athens we were warmly greeted by the Greek people, flowers were thrown at the trucks by laughing lasses and the troops scrambled onto the roof, running boards and mudguards of the trucks to cheer and wave back to the friendly Greeks.

The Rebels and Horrie were among the occupants of one particular truck. Horrie, very excited, was hoisted up onto the roof of the truck and barked his reply to the laughing people. Someone among the crowd who lined the footpaths would spot Horrie and excitedly draw the attention of others who laughed and waved to the little excited pup.

Their wave of greeting was entirely unlike that of our own, they extended the hand out with the palm turned up, closing and opening the hand in the manner of a beckon rather than a wave. We were later told that the meaning was 'Go and return'. "Wish we were the last truck in the convoy," remarked Don. "A flat tyre would be welcome right now," replied Fitz. Murchie, balancing precariously on the cabin roof, waved his rifle to the call of 'Benghazi Benghazi' from the crowd. Apparently the fall of Benghazi to the Australian troops was still fresh in the memory of the Greek people. Murchie acknowledged and accepted the entire credit.

The reception we received was fitting for conquering heroes, perhaps they realised the task ahead of us better than we did, but we returned not as conquering heroes. Our best was given most willingly but the story of David and Goliath is not repeated in modern warfare when it is man against machines. What little consolation we had after our withdrawal, was that we had left behind us more dead and smashed enemy than the entire number of our small force and the curtain has not yet been rung down on the true ending of the battle for Greece.

Leaving the outskirts of Athens we commenced the first stage of the northward journey by road to the front, as we cleared the outskirts of Athens we looked back and high up on a hill we could see the famous ruins of the Acropolis overlooking the city. Passing through numerous villages the welcome was the same, each village had its own church with a high steeple and each village its village square, in the centre of the square stood a white wooden cross symbolic of the crucifixion. Quaint square white-washed houses lined the narrow winding cobbled streets. Often there was just sufficient room for a vehicle the size of an army truck to pass through.

The windows of the dwellings above the shops that also lined the streets were crowded with cheering laughing people. Horrie on the truck roof, always the centre of attention and delight. The narrow foot-paths that lined the road were overcrowded with cheering villagers, many in their national costumes. The village lasses were a picture, jet black straight hair, laughing brown eyes and smooth olive skin They wore white ankle length flared out skirts embroidered with designs of flowers of contrasting colours, white lacy blouses pulled in tight at the waist with little vests of vivid blue or red, laced crisscross down the front with a silk chord, wide puffy sleeves caught in tight above the elbows, and tiny sandaled feet peeped out from the generous skirts.

The men folk wore long sheepskin coats and black velvet trousers caught in below the knee after the style of 'bowyangs' and the head gear a skull cap like our own old fashioned night caps. Also here and there we noticed Greek priests clothed in ankle-length black flowing gowns and most wore a short beard.

Every few miles we noticed a small white box mounted on a post on the roadside, this little white washed box was in the shape like a slanting roof letter box. Although the glass front of the box could be seen, a lamp burning at the foot of a miniature crucifix and also inside, a painting of St. Francis, the traveller's Patron Saint. (Not sure if I have got the right Saint.) The box also contained money in a small till. The miniature shrine was to enable any traveller the opportunity of worship and if necessary the money could be taken to enable him to buy food as he travelled the road.

These peaceful symbols typical of kindly warm hearted people were soon to witness the vicious mighty strength of the advancing Nazi army.

The first night we camped off the road on the side of a small rocky hill, the hillside was covered with bramble and generously sprinkled with poppies and small white wild flowers. In the valley at the foot of the hill flowed a small crystal clear stream over a bed of pure white round pebbles, and along the bank on either side the slight breeze rippled small fields of green and golden barley.

It was a beautiful country and during the night the Rebels were unusually quiet as they listened to the tinkling of bells that were attached to the necks of small flocks of sheep and goats that roamed the hill.

The following morning we travelled on and up through the Thermo-pylae pass, the road continually winding around. At the top we halted for a few minutes to view the magnificent scene below. Nine separate sections of the road were visible, each a different height, and far below the cultivated patches and fields appeared like a giant chess board. Gleaming silver in the light, a long stretch of road divided the chess board as it ran from the bottom of the pass into the town of Lamia. As we progressed further north we had expected to encounter hostile aircraft but we eventually reached the foot of Mt Olympus without sighting any planes. Later we found that the reason for the absence of planes was due to the excessive rains that had hopelessly bogged the enemy airfields.

We established Battalion Headquarters at the foot of Mt Olympus. Mt Olympus rose some 9,600 feet and only seldom could one glimpse the snow-capped peak as it gleamed through the purple haze.

At the foot of Mt Olympus the rebel section were split up. Fitz and Gordie were to remain temporarily at Btn HQ doing signal duties. Feathers went out with A Company in charge of a section of attached Signallers. Murchie was given the job of Spotter riding on the running board of the Adjutant's car. Poppa took over the duties of Signal Officer and Signal Sergeant as well. Don and I were to be used as Despatch riders between Btn HQ and Company HQ under Corporal Roy Thurgood, undoubtedly one of the best Despatch Rider's in Greece. Poppa worked like a Trojan, spending countless hours supervising Signal Communications. D Company moved on out to the Albanian border and A, B and C Companies moved out to join two Australian and one New Zealand Brigades that were in position defending Servia Pass.

The German artillery had the range to the pass down to a nicety and during the day and night the pass was continually under artillery fire, it was given the name Hellfire Pass by the troops.

The southern approach to the pass was along a fairly straight road and during the day hostile aircraft hovered above this straight, screaming down every now and then to strafe the trucks and Despatch R's that scooted up the straight hell for leather to gain the little protection that the 'S' bend afforded.

The village of Servia had been razed to the ground by the constant bombing. The road itself passed the village and although the pass was in a pretty bad state, shell and bomb craters were numerous alongside the actual road; dust from the craters had been falling across the road and the frequent rain and passing of many vehicles bringing up supplies had turned the road into a muddy nightmare.

On the day that I took Horrie through the pass all the remaining Rebels at Btn HQ's were away on various jobs and I did not wish to bother anyone else to look after Horrie while I was away, although plenty would have gladly looked after the pup.

My instructions were clear enough but little did I realise that the trip was to be so bad for the little wog dog. I struck the straight road that approached the pass without incident and as the road was muddy I proceeded along at a cautious pace, Horrie was popped inside the front of my greatcoat, a belt around the waist prevented him from slipping down.

Unfortunately I struck the road when it was deserted, otherwise I would have had warning from the Spotters riding on the trucks. A sudden roar above my head told me the worst, I had been spotted from above, the noise from my cycle prevented me from getting any warning until the plane was horribly close, little pieces of mud flicked up alongside and continued up along the road ahead.

I laid the cycle over on its side and the cycle, Horrie and I slid into the ditch alongside of the road as the first plane zoomed, the second appeared, and clutching Horrie I hugged the mud and held my breath. Three planes in all joined in the sport. Horrie kicked frantically, badly scared by the spill and the noise of the planes. After the third had zoomed up I followed the line of flight, they were now climbing in a very suggestive looking circle.

I was scrambling to get the tangle of Horrie, myself and the cycle sorted out as a truck pulled up sharply. The driver called "Are you alright Dig?" "I think so," I replied hopefully. "Make for the pass like hell, they'll be back in a minute!" he advised and the truck whizzed off. I managed to get the cycle started and looking for the planes I noticed them climbing and turning away out to my left. I had about half a mile of straight road to travel before reaching the pass. 'Still... still... Good dog, good dog,' quietened Horrie and flat out we made for the pass, but no hope. Horrie and I made for the ditch again, this time on my feet hugging the mud again. I counted the roar of the three planes as they roared past. Horrie struggled violently again but I sat up after the third had passed: 'Poor little pup... Good little dog' and the tail wagged again. The three planes continued in a straight line. Thank Christ, I muttered to myself.

Horrie was quickly gaining confidence but like myself he was mud from head to foot. We gained the pass without further incident. Just after passing Lamia village I was halted by one of the road patrol. "They are shelling the pass again," he informed me, "Been through before?" "No," I replied. "Well, here's the drum (good oil)… get close up to the second bend, wait until you see the flash, then beat it through before they get the second away, don't worry about the first, it'll be as quick as the flash. Where'd you get the pup?" "At the first flash," I replied having a one track mind. "Not scared are you?" he asked a little anxiously. "No." I lied.

I reached the second bend and pulled up alongside a stationary truck, the driver was standing by the side of the road, I walked over to him, "How's she going Dig?" I enquired. "The first over," came the answer followed by a deep explosion over the embankment to our right.

He dived into the ditch and I followed suit. "This one should be in the I diddle-diddle," (middle) he informed me. Fortunately it was not quite in the middle but landed over the embankment to our left. "We're Jake (okay) now for a bit," he remarked getting to his feet, "Although you can't bank on it, Jerry is using a pretty big mortar over there and occasionally whips in a fourth for good measure," he continued. While lying in the ditch I had been holding my hands over the outside of my greatcoat to keep Horrie quiet and my muddy friend noticed the swelling in the front for the first time.

Taking Horrie from beneath my coat he still had a wag for the driver who patted him. "Look Dig," he said "The road is knocked about pretty badly around the next bend, better let me take the pup in the truck and I'll pick you up at the end of the pass." Thankfully I accepted the offer and Horrie disappeared into the cabin of the truck.

The truck was first away and Horrie had scrambled on the driver's lap and looked out the window to see if I was following, sighting me a little way behind he barked his encouragement as I slithered and slid up the road. 'Whiz' overhead, they had started again, but we were through the pass.

As I pulled up alongside the truck, Horrie, not waiting to be let out of the cabin jumped from the window. "That little bloke was worried about you," laughed the driver, "Well good luck Dig." "Ok thanks a lot, she's right," and we parted.

I located B Company and completed my job. Locating the Signallers, I found Nippy Bourke, Bill Arrowsmith and Ron Baker the Sig. truck drivers together. Ron readily agreed to take Horrie back to Btn HQ on his return trip. Nippy relayed an amusing incident that had happened a little time previously. He and Bill Arrowsmith had set their telephone up at the base of a huge olive tree. However a sudden attack from low flying aircraft strafing the area had set Nippy and Bill scooting around the tree for shelter. Unfortunately, one went each side and they met violently at the back.

Bill sported a busted nose and Nippy had a lump on his head like a cricket ball. Ron Baker who had witnessed the incident from another tree stopped laughing when he felt a tug on the tail of his coat. Examination showed a little round hole.

Ron Baker and Horrie got away and through the pass without any trouble but on the straight stretch they had to make several scrambles for shelter. Fearing Horrie may not return when called, Ron had carried the pup on each occasion. I overtook the truck just as it entered the track that lead through the bushy and tree covered area of Btn HQ's. Ron had to hold Horrie with one hand to prevent him from jumping out of the cabin window when he noticed me alongside the truck. After scraping off the worst of the mud, I visited the Cook's and returned to Horrie and Don, picking out some of the meat for Horrie, we both forgot the pass.

That night Murchie came in again and related some of the experiences he had up through the pass. Horrie listened closely but offered no comment.

Later Poppa came over and informed us Fitz and Gordie had gone out to replace two Sigs that had been knocked, we were sorry to hear that Harry Doran and Mat Taylor had been hit. "Rotten luck. They were good blokes both of them," remarked Murchie.

Don and I had made a little shelter from our gas capes and water proof ground sheets, there was just sufficient room to crawl in under the cover and Horrie crawled in with us and slept at our feet.

That night we decided that if there were none of us able to look after Horrie, we would give him to Doc Sholto Douglas, our M.D. as we knew he would keep an eye on Horrie. Although he was kept busy he was one of Horrie's firm friends.

The morning found the top of our shelter crisp with ice and long after Don and I turned out, Horrie remained well hidden under the warmth of the blankets. Poppa was away on a cycle bright and early. He returned before lunch with a passenger behind him. Dropping the passenger into the R.A.P. he helped him into the tent. "Who did you bring in?" I enquired as we had seen the incident only from a distance. "Yugoslav," replied Poppa, "Picked him up this side of the pass. Leg pretty badly mangled." Later we found out Poppa's so-called Yugoslav wore a little crooked cross beneath the pocket of his tunic. Poppa only grinned.

Doc Douglas treated the German and he was removed in an ambulance. Having a job to do I walked over to the bushes where my cycle was concealed and rode back to Don and Horrie. On my way out, Horrie struggled in Don's arms, he was quite ready for another run on the cycle.

When the withdrawal commenced it was our job to keep the trucks moving, riding up and down the long convoy, sorting out tangles, directing turn offs, etc. Ray Thurgood worked like a tiger. It was pretty hard work on that greasy muddy road and he set an example that I will always remember. We did not see Fitz and Gordie again until we arrived in Crete.

By the time our withdrawal commenced, Greek soldiers were drifting back from Albania. They were in a pitiable condition, often rags wound round their feet replaced boots long since worn out, unwashed, unshaven and almost exhausted, they staggered in ones and twos and little groups along the road. Whenever possible we piled them onto the already overloaded trucks and their gratitude for tins of bully beef and army biscuits was pitiable to see.

Many carried rifles of the single shot variety and what little equipment they had was poor and out of date. These were the men who so thoroughly thrashed the Italians in Albania, in spite of the Italian modern equipment.

Along the road also struggled old men, women and children carrying what few scanty belongings they could. The troops threw bully beef and biscuits to them but unfortunately we were unable to help them all. They still retained their friendly wave but their faces were grim and set.

Pulling up for a brief spell alongside a cottage I noticed an elderly woman trying to dig a hole alongside the stone wall that surrounded the cottages. Too old to join the throng of people who had left their homes and were struggling south, while our small stopping force bitterly contested every inch as they fell back under the mighty pressure; this poor old soul was trying to hide the tins of bully beef that the troops had thrown into her cottage garden. "Devourie, Devourie," she said and pointed towards the north. Hastily I did the job for her.

When I looked around she was sitting on the edge of the stone wall in the yard and holding Horrie in her arms. In spite of his distrust for strangers he lay quietly and contented. Propping the spade against the stone wall I crossed over to her and taking the pup, put him inside my coat, his little head popped out between the buttons. With tears streaming down her kindly wrinkled old face she put one hand on my arm and one on Horrie's head and mumbled something. Not daring to look up I noticed Horrie lick her hand. "God protect you," I muttered and without looking back and moved on.

Raid after raid harassed the convoy forcing troops to take shelter off the road, often when they returned to the trucks after the planes had passed it was only to find many of them destroyed and burning. These trucks had to be pushed off the road as often there was no room to detour.

Men worked like maniacs, there must be no hold up. Others had to get out too, and were depending on those in front to keep moving. Personnel from ruined vehicles clambered aboard other trucks wherever possible and the convoy moved on leaving A Company defending the battered airfield outside Larissa. The convoy moved on to where it was halted outside the town of Larissa. After a terrific pounding the occupants of Larissa were graciously given three hours to evacuate the town.

The convoy halted in order to allow the occupants of Larissa to move out in all haste without the hindrance of vehicles moving on the roads through town. At the railway station to the right of the town stood a tram, already hopelessly overcrowded.

I passed numerous people and children hurrying towards the station while high up overhead three Jerry planes hovered like birds of prey. Passing through the town, to the right and between the Station and main centre of the township, I passed about thirty small girls all dressed alike in white. They moved in an orderly manner towards the railway station, six children walked in front carrying a white sheet quartered by a broad red cross, one child held each corner and one each side of the middle. The party was in the charge of five nuns, so I gathered they were children from a convent somewhere in Larissa. They showed no signs of panic or fear and several little hands fluttered as I passed. Surely such little children carrying the symbol of mercy had nothing to fear.

Outside Larissa to the south, the road had been raised up some five feet above a long stretch of flat swampy ground. The surface of the road through rain and the passing of numerous vehicles was an absolute driver's nightmare.

Continually a flight of German planes policed the bad stretch of about one mile. Trucks were unable to move faster than 5mph and even then the back wheels continually slithered from side to side. Once off the road and down the slippery incline it was impossible to regain the narrow road surface.

Palestinian troops worked like demons on this bad stretch filling in craters almost as soon as they appeared. There was no cover of any description and the trucks just had to take it as the planes dived time and time again on the convoy. Soldiers endeavoured to return the fire with small arms but the crowded moving trucks did not afford much help.

After strafing the convoy the planes flew low over Larissa using the remainder of their ammunition before returning to their airfields to reload.

Checking the number of trucks passed in my section I noticed one missing and I returned through Larissa to locate the stray truck. I passed the shocking sight of the little bodies of the children in white, they lay scattered where they fell, like broken trodden and crushed little red and white roses. An Australian ambulance was in attendance but few were left to remember their playmates, strafed and killed while bearing the Red Cross by those yellow nosed planes, flown by such inhumane fiendish bastards of Goering's Luftwaffe.

God only knows how we crossed that mad muddy mile. I remember only time and time again the front wheel stopping, choked with mud tightly wedged between the mudguard and the wheel; often smoke issued from the tyres caused by the friction between the rubber tyre and the tightly packed mud. During one of these halts Don came up alongside and between us we managed to bend upwards the section of mudguard that protruded out of the front wheel, so enabling the front wheel to turn more freely. Horrie all this time remained quite still inside my coat, his little head poked out between two buttons. 'Good little dog,' I tried to reassure him that all was well. He was far more reassured than I was feeling.

Eventually we got across and continued along the road towards Lamia. Before dusk we turned off the main road and prepared to camp for the night in a small valley surrounded on three sides by rocky hills.

Trucks dispersed over the area and bleary eyed drivers sought to rest under and alongside their trucks. Just on dusk a flight of hostile aircraft flew low over the area, our light Ack-Ack Bren guns opened up on them but the fire was not returned and we were left in peace.

I pulled in alongside Ron Baker's truck and poor little Horrie was allowed to stretch his legs. He was as game as ever and trotted off to investigate the bushes on the side of the hill. Every now and then he answered the call of the boys, who called him to offer little tit bits of bully beef and to pat the game little wog dog.

I had arranged to meet Don at Ron Baker's truck as we were to sleep under it at night. I had been riding near the head of the Company convoy and Don near the rear. When darkness fell with no sign of Don, Poppa came over and together with Ron Baker and Reg Jenks we went back to the turnoff. Two trucks were also missing, and it was apparent they had missed the turnoff into our camping area. We could only hope that they might as darkness fell, pull onto the side of the road and try and pick us up in the morning.

Dog tired we returned to the trucks to get a little rest. After darkness fell, little fires appeared in the hills surrounding the area where we had camped. In all probability these fires were lit to disclose our position to the enemy. They were quickly extinguished when we fired an anti-tank rifle in their direction.

Horrie snuggled up close to me and we slept soundly until Poppa awoke me at 2am, as it was my turn to piquet the section of trucks in our area until 4am. Scarcely able to keep my eyes open I sat on a rock some fifty yards up the hill from the trucks.

My mind continually went back to the little children in Larissa and to Don's absence. Horrie sat between my legs and a growl from the pup brought me back to the surroundings with a start. "What is it Horrie?" softly from me. In answer he took a few paces up the hill, stopped and growled again.

Remembering the fires earlier in the evening, I quietly lowered myself to the ground to try and silhouette the short distance to the hill top against the sky.

I put my hand on Horrie and felt him quivering, and he growled again. I was only able to make out the dim outline of rocks against the sky, but Horrie was insistent and advanced towards a vague dim object some thirty feet away.

Calling to Horrie to stand fast I flanked out to the right as the object of Horrie's attention was a little above me. Cautiously I moved up until on about a level with Horrie and slowly moved in and up to the left. Horrie hearing my approach waited no longer and growling earnestly he darted at the vague object on the ground.

The dark object rose up quickly from the ground and remained perfectly still at my call of 'Halt!' Horrie ran back to me and remained at my feet facing and growling at the stranger.

I called to 'Advance one pace but no more!' He replied "Kalini-hta" (Greek for goodnight). Taking no chance I moved in close enough to motion him towards the camp, Horrie growled at his heels while I manoeuvred him to the OC truck. The OC, Captain Plumes sent for the Greek cook who was with our Company.

After being interrogated, it seemed he was a Greek shepherd looking for goats that had strayed from his flock over the hill. Surprised, he sighted the trucks and heard the dog growl, afraid of being discovered near the camp and mistaken for a fifth columnist he had laid down hoping to avoid detection.

The story seemed plausible and he was escorted from the camp and permitted to return to his flock. The remainder of my watch was uneventful, I sat down and talked quietly to Horrie "You little trimmer," I said gently stroking his head, he turned and licked my hand, man's most faithful friend.

In the early morning daylight I searched the spot over the hill, there were no signs of goats or any other animals having been in that vicinity.

Moving again we continued towards Lamia, time and time again the convoy was held up by herds of cattle on the road, there could be no delay and the trucks pushed through the cattle, many poor beasts were sent crashing down the steep banks to the ravine far below. Later we were informed these incidents were deliberate attempts to delay the convoys, the shepherds were fifth columnists.

Passing through one small village I noticed a commotion. It appeared that an elderly man had been sitting by the roadside apparently reading a paper. The curiosity of a Greek woman had been aroused and she stopped our R.S.U. Kelly. Kelly approached the man who noticed the approach and turned and ran, Kelly dropped him with a stone.

Greek soldiers who were in the village took charge and it was found that the man had been checking the trucks through the village while pretending to be reading the paper. Checking the paper it was found that he had made a very thorough check as the serial no's of the trucks, their type and approximate numbers of soldiers they contained had been written down. He was shot on the spot by Greek soldiers.

Lamia was blanketed under a pall of smoke, here too the German planes had been busy. Buildings had crashed across the street and small parties of Greek men and women worked to clear the debris from the road to enable us to pass through, fires burned fiercely, choking fumes and dust from crumbled masonry made breathing difficult.

Further through the town the carnage was ghastly, bewildered old people wandered aimlessly through the street, small terrified children scrambled among the bundles that lay grotesquely everywhere, the screams of the hurt and dying were answered by the mournful wailing of sirens. The planes were returning.

We camped again that night along the bank of a small stream some little distance from Lamia. No sign of Don or the missing trucks had been seen all day. Once again troops were in position at Thermopylae pass but the Greek collapse had left a way for the German forces to work into the rear of the Thermopylae position from Yannina.

Fitz and Gordie were reported to be okay. Feathers was still with A Company but Don and Murchie were missing. Poppa was still intact but had a painfully bruised shoulder owing to a spill from his cycle in Lamia, I was told later that he purposely hit a heap of rubble in order to dodge a terrified child who had run across his path.

My cycle was required by the Provost Cops who were trying to keep some sort of order in Lamia and keep the convoys moving. From here on I travelled with Ron Baker as relief driver, Horrie took a good view of travelling in the cabin of the truck.

Daylight and the Luftwaffe arrived together but Horrie, hearing the planes before us, woke us in time to seek shelter. Before laying down to sleep the previous night, we had dug shallow trenches, and fortunately we were able to take cover while the area received heavy machine gunning.

One bomb fell in the camp area and Bert Bottom scrambled into the crater and mounted a Bren gun in the German made shelter. Jim Averill and Fred Richardson quickly joined him and they had plenty of targets to choose from, they put up a remarkably fine effort.

After the raid the only casualty was a poor old donkey that had been feeding quietly along the bank of the creek. After the planes had passed, Horrie received plenty of praise and tit bits for his timely warning. He accepted our small offering and words of praise: 'Good little dog, very smart pup', with much tail wagging. Shortly after the raid we were moving again.

The morning of April 24th found us hidden in an olive grove some little distance from the village of Mandra. We were to remain hidden during the day and move again at night.

At about midday Poppa, Horrie and I walked up through the village. Approaching a Café we noticed parked outside a battered old truck alongside the kerb. It was partly burnt and riddled like a sieve.

A roar of laughter from inside the Café drifted out to us followed by an unsteady voice singing the 6th Divvy song 'Old Blamey's Boys'. As Poppa and I walked towards the door of the Café the song continued:

Old Blamey's boys, 6th Divvy boys,
fighting for Victory, Liberty, Democracy,
Oh Hitler we warn, we're the A.I.F reborn,
and like good old Gunga Din, we can take it on the chin,
cause we're Old Blamey's Boys.

We entered and beheld none other than Murchie standing unsteadily on a little table beating time to the tune with a bottle of Vino in his hand. "Wog dog!" he called, sighting Poppa, Horrie and I, "You little dasher!" (beauty). Two Kiwis helped him down from the table while I picked Horrie up and we pushed our way through the Greek soldiers who were crowded around the table from where Murchie was being helped down. "Struth!" exclaimed Poppa, "What a sight…"

Murchie wore an Officer's cap, anything up to eight days growth of beard, a German Lugar pistol on one side of his waist belt and a wicked looking knife thrust through the other, while across his shoulder was slung a Tommy gun. Shaking hands excitedly, Murchie then took Horrie from my arms, and he endeavoured to lick Murchie's bearded face, "Wog dog!" he called again, lifting Horrie up above his head for all the laughing Greeks to admire.

The Café owner pushed his way through the crowd and motioned to us to follow him. He lead us to a table the Greeks had cleared for us. Being seated at the table, Murchie said, "Vino, Vino for the mob George!" waving his hand around in a circle. He introduced the two Kiwis to us "Archie, Bash, meet Poppa, Jim and Horrie the wog dog, cobbers of mine" he exclaimed.

Glasses filled all round, he pulled an expensive looking gold wrist watch from his pocket; "Cut this out in Vino, George." George the Café owner smiled and nodded his head putting the watch in his pocket at the same time. Turning to us Murchie explained, "German officer gave it to me." The two Kiwis laughed. "Wait a bit Murchie!" I exclaimed, "Hang on to the watch, Poppa and I can pay for this." "She's right," he replied,"Got another here," patting his pocket.

He removed his tunic and folding it, placed it in the centre of the table and sat Horrie down on it. "Glass top tables too cold for wog dogs," he explained. Calling George he ordered a glass of milk for Horrie, going through the motions of milking. Between numerous glasses of vino we learnt that he got mixed up during a hectic race for shelter off the road, returning after the raid he found his own vehicle destroyed and he clambered aboard one of the Kiwi's trucks.

The Kiwis unit had been knocked about pretty badly and in the confusion Murchie, Archie and Bash managed to get the old discarded truck going and set out for Lamia. They filled the truck with Greek soldiers and followed the convoy south and eventually found their way to Mandra. He had no idea that part of our unit were only about half a mile from the Café.

The Greek soldiers Murchie explained, would come in handy if the evacuation 'came unstuck' as with their help we might be able to hang out in the hills until we find some way of getting back to Egypt.

"There must be plenty of small fishing craft around the coast that we can commandeer," he continued. Poppa and I agreed that it was worth a shot anyway.

Archie and Bash were told about the little dogs adventures and Horrie received plenty of attention from them. Horrie looked across at me and wagged his tail: 'these blokes are alright' his expression said.

A Greek soldier came over to our table and excitedly exclaimed "Turkey bomb bomb German." Turkey at war with Germany we gathered. This was extra good news.

"Do you think it possible that Turkey could cut the German line of communication between Albania, Yugoslavia and Greece?" Archie inquired. "It would be a good show if she could," replied Poppa "If the British could get more troops and equipment over to us here we might get the Hun between two fires." "But," I remarked;"The Greeks have already capitulated to the Huns." "So What!" came from the door. "Don!" Murchie, Poppa and I exclaimed together unable to believe our eyes, we rushed over to him all asking questions together, Horrie bounded down from the table and joined us. "Alright, Alright take it easy," said Don picking Horrie up.

We pulled another chair up to the table and filled one glass full from the several partly filled glasses in front of us. "Swig it down and start talking," advised Poppa. "You might introduce me to your friends," smiled Don. "Sorry you blokes," I answered,"This is Archie and Bash, Don." "Well," said Don, "first of all Feathers is okay and at the moment asleep in one of the trucks, with a little luck Fitz and Gordie will pull in before we move off again tonight." "Think we had better get tight on the strength of it," replied Poppa, already tight. "What the hell happened to you?" I asked.

Don told his story: "After we got over that bad patch outside Larissa, I pulled up for a spell but after a few minutes rest I was unable to get the cycle moving. It took me half an hour to get it going, by this time several more convoys pulled in behind you. I passed quite a few trucks and was hoping to eventually overtake you, however after a fair while I realised that I should have caught up with you by this time and that you could scarcely still be ahead of me. It was getting dark so I sat in behind a convoy of New Zealanders and when they stopped I camped with them for the night.

"They were to try and pass through Lamia the next morning so I reckoned it safer to stay with them, and so if I could find out whether you had passed through Lamia or not from the Provost there. I got in touch with a Provost in Lamia, he could not recall the serial no's of our trucks but told me a large convoy had passed along the coast road. "Had Lamia been bombed?" I asked. "Not very heavily the first time I went through but let me finish..." he replied. "I continued along the coast road to Volos and as I entered Volos I picked up Eddie White, our

Transport Officer, Provost Brown and Leo Colman, one of the Don R's out with Lt. White trying to locate some missing trucks so I joined in with them. After passing through Volos we cut back towards the mountains again and completed a circle finishing up again in Lamia. This time Lamia had been 'done over' properly.

"Lt. White contacted the Provost again and found that while we were making the circle you had followed us, but apparently instead of cutting back towards the mountains you had continued along the coast road towards Corinth. We simply followed you up and located the trucks at the olive grove about half an hour ago. Reg Jenks told me Feathers and A Co. Signals had pulled in but Feather's was all in and having a rest. You and Poppa had told Reg that you would be back about 1.30pm, but as it was then 3.30pm, I guessed where I might find you, but little did I think that I would find Murchie with you!" I explained to Don how he had missed us after we turned off the Lamia road to camp for the night.

"What about your outfit?" I asked Archie and Bash. "Guess they are split up all over the place," they replied. "If it's okay, we will tag along with you until we can locate them again.""That should be okay," replied Poppa "Did you hear anything about Turkey being at war with Germany?" I asked Don. "Yes," he replied, "They have got it at the camp also but no one seems to know if it's correct or not." "What about the Greeks?" I asked Murchie. "Let them have the truck and they can follow us when we pull out tonight," he replied.

We eventually made them understand and setting them up with some rations we parked the battered old truck near our own lines, bidding them to follow when we pulled out after dark.

Shortly after dark we were under way again, news had been received that German airborne troops were expected to land at Corinth and try to cut our retreat by blowing the canal bridge.

The race commenced to get the convoy through before daylight. Trucks used their headlights now and hundreds of headlights could be seen moving at different levels down the mountainside as we approached

Corinth. We passed through Corinth at night and now headed for Argos which is way south of Corinth. Paratroops were dropped and the main bridge to Athens was blown in the morning but the convoy was through.

Just before daylight we pulled into another little olive grove to hide from the planes for the day, we searched for the Greek soldiers but were unable to locate them. "Probably had trouble with the old truck," suggested Archie. We found the truck that Feathers was with, but were unable to find Fitz or Gordie. Poppa enquired if we knew what day it was but we had not the slightest idea. "April 25th Anzac Day!" he declared. I recalled some remarks about Anzac day and Poppa way back in Egypt, those days now seemed like years. "Let's wander up through the village and see if we can get a spot of Vino," suggested Murchie.

On our way to the village we passed numerous trucks hidden away among the olive trees. Soldiers were digging shelter holes at the foot of the trees. Before long the planes would be over again searching for and machine gunning troops where the presence of soldiers was suspected.

Horrie scampered around investigating bushes and trees, then he would scamper back to us full of beans and fun. Poppa was very quiet, we realised that this Anzac day spent hiding and running away from the enemy contrasted with that memorable Anzac Day Poppa had seen on Gallipoli.

"Cheer up Poppa," I advised "It's not all over yet!" "I know," he replied "But it stinks a bit." "I'd rather stop with the Greeks than beat it," remarked Murchie. The Rebels were quiet for a while, I guessed they were thinking as I was, of the old people and children we were to leave behind. "Perhaps we may come back some day?" remarked Don. "I'll be in that," replied Feathers. "Me too!" we all replied including the two Kiwis.

We strolled into a village, the Greek folk were all out in the street talking in little groups, they smiled at us as we passed. "For God's sake let's get a drink," said Poppa. Finding a little deserted Café we sat down at a table to be served vino, pooling our cash we made Poppa the treasurer. A commotion outside in the street accompanied by Horrie's bark brought us to the door.

Horrie, who had investigated a cottage on the other side of the street had bumped into a very annoyed fowl and proud mother of a scared brood. He very reluctantly returned when I called him and picking him up I returned with the Rebels into the shop.

Not long after we had settled down at the table an elderly woman rather timidly approached us from the doorway. She was carrying a brace of trussed-up fowls. Smiling, she presented them to me while Don held the eager pup. "For you, for you," she said in English. Poppa thrust a handful of money into her protesting hand but we were so insistent that she had to reluctantly accept the money. Smiling, she beckoned us to accompany her across the road to a humble cottage. We followed her, Don carrying Horrie and I carrying the trussed-up fowls.

The cottage was a small square rough stone structure. Over the door stood an archway covered with grapevine, it stood out clean and cool looking against the background of the white washed stone wall. Heading us into the dining room she motioned us to be seated at a large table. The dining room was exceptionally large and seemed to occupy the most part of the square cottage.

The room was conspicuously clean and the furniture obviously home-made, was sturdy and comfortable. On the mantlepiece above a large open fire place I noticed a bronze figure of a crucifix and on the wall above a picture of the Mother Mary. Although the room was clean and bright, an atmosphere of sorrow seemed to exist and to speak one felt the desire to whisper softly and I felt rough and clumsy. The spell was broken by the old lady returning into the room with a bottle of vino and glasses, brown bread and white sour cheese made from goats milk were placed before us and a glass bowl of gherkins in olive oil. Smiling our thanks we ate the offering, her kind face beamed with pleasure as she fussed around us.

Presently she disappeared again and returned with a small photo of two Greek soldiers, showing it to each of us in turn we asked if it was father and son. Her face reflected pride and sorrow. Taking the photo she closed her eyes and inclined her head on her hand; Albania, Italian, we made out.

Her husband and son asleep in Albania, left to carry on alone soon she must witness the spreading disease of German's putrefying the very air with their breathing in this clean tidy country.

Taking our leave we made our way back along the winding narrow street in the direction of our camping area. A short distance from the cottage her voice calling made us turn, she had discovered the trussed fowls that I had left behind. Afraid of offending her, we accepted the gift. We roasted the fowls over a small fire. "Anzac Day..." said Poppa, bitterly. Horrie enjoyed his share with a few growls of approval.

Before we left again that night all the blankets we could find and rations we could scrounge were taken to her little cottage of sorrow and loneliness and quietly placed on the doorway beneath the vine covered arch.

We arrived at Kalamata early next morning, all throughout that day troops poured into the area; Tommies, Australians, New Zealanders, Greeks and Yugoslavs, this was to be the last organised stand in Greece. That night the British navy was to make the last attempt to get the remaining troops off. The evacuation had been masterly timed and all now depended on the British navy.

Thousands of trucks were destroyed, oil and water drained from the engines, the motors raced dry until they seized, tyres slashed and all conceivable damage done except burning as the fires would have betrayed our position to the planes.

All day long great Sunderland's were evacuating wounded from the beach. It was uncanny how they missed the Luftwaffe who almost continually flew overhead bombing and machine gunning areas where they suspected the presence of troops. Everything of any possible use was given to the villagers, Greek men and women worked on the roads filling in craters, advising where troops could best be concealed, weeping girls clung to soldiers imploring them to take them away before the Germans arrived. I noticed two girls in Australian soldier's uniforms seeking to make a desperate bid for freedom; they were seen again on our transport ship so probably they got to Crete, from the frying pan into the fire.

Greek families packed goods on donkeys and set out for the hills, soldiers sought friends in various units, often to receive the worst news. Don, Horrie and I stood by the roadside and watched for some old friends from the 1st Anti-Tank Regiment. We found a few but many were never to be seen again.

Someone in a crowded truck noticed Horrie "Stick to him Digger!" the soldier called. The faces of the soldiers were bitter in defeat but a great lesson in courage had been learnt from the Greek people.

The Destroyer *Defender* ferried us out to the troopship *Costa Rica*. Archie, Bash, Poppa and the Rebels were together waiting for the destroyer to take us off, but in the dense crowd we became separated, not collecting again until we arrived in Crete.

The morning found the troopships sailing in line abreast, the *Costa Rica* (our ship) occupied the left flank, the *City of London* the centre position and the *Delwarra* the right flank, the Escorts, Destroyers *Defender*, *Hero* and *Hereward* and Ack-Ack Cruiser *Calcutta.*

During the first attack I noticed Don in the crowd that lined the side of the ship to get a few rounds away at the planes. I led Horrie up out of the way and joined him. Soldiers appeared carrying large dishes procured from somewhere within the ship: "Pool your arms boys!" they called.

Never has there been a contribution given so readily to a common fund, all down the deck they carried the dishes of rounds, soldiers contributing here, others receiving there. It was a good idea, not one single rifle was idle. Some of the crew appeared with buckets of tea, there was no panic at all, in fact the troops brightened considerably.

This was a chance to hit back after the days of hiding, unable to fire in fear of betraying positions and so lose valuable trucks necessary to get the troops to Kalamata. Later Don and I became separated again while trying to get below for a feed and did not meet up again until Crete.

The destroyer *Defender* took Horrie and myself to Crete after the sinking of the *Costa Rica*. Landing at Souda Bay during an air raid, Horrie and I sought cover in a narrow road cutting. While waiting there Poppa and Don arrived. After the raid we moved to a transit camp that had hastily been formed to sort out troops returning from Greece, to their various units. It was at this camp just outside the town of Chania that we met up again with Fitz, Gordie, Feathers and Murchie. They were all overjoyed at seeing Horrie safe and sound.

We received a good hot meal at this camp and the little party of Rebels sat down together under an olive tree to enjoy the feed and talk over the various incidents we experienced in Greece. Horrie made short work of the feed that was given to him and leaving him in the care of the Rebels, I returned to the place where food was being dished out in effort to secure more food for Horrie. On my way back to the Rebels, Les Jeffers told me he had rescued Horrie from the *Costa Rica* and had been keeping the dog until he found me to hand him over.

Les Jeffers, a lad from NSW joined our unit shortly before we left Egypt for Greece. He knew Fitz and Gordie fairly well and conse-quently knew Horrie slightly; the dog he produced was something like Horrie and the mistake he made was quite understandable.

During the scramble to get off the *Costa Rica* Les had noticed this little dog on deck and picking it up he carried it with him. Some of the lads later told us that it was a pet of the *Costa Rica* crew, the Rebels kept the dog hoping to locate some of the ship's crew and so give it back to them but we were unsuccessful. I fancy the crew were taken from Crete to Egypt very shortly after they were collected again. We named this new member Horrietta as she was a bitch. With the exception of the sandy streak along the back her colouring was the same as Horrie's.

Her head was very much like Horrie's except that her ears were never cocked as Horrie's were on occasions. She also had a long tail, the little dog had been well cared for and she was very fond of being petted. Horrietta became very attached to Horrie and she would follow him everywhere he went. Horrie in turn was a little jealous if he considered she was receiving too much attention from the Rebels.

Horrietta had been taught to sit up much to Horrie's interest, unable to get the purchase that she could with her long tail. As Murchie advised him; 'He wasn't in the race.' We tried to teach him and he was very keen to learn but the moment we let him go he would overbalance.

During the first bombing raid we experienced, Horrietta was pathetically frightened and she trembled violently for a long while afterwards in spite of our efforts to soothe her. Had we been unsuccessful in finding a home for her, we decided it would be much better if we shot her if the works were going to be turned on heavily again.

During these violent tremors Horrie himself would try and soothe her, he would lick her face and prance about endeavouring to get her to play but his efforts were also unsuccessful. Arch and Bash came over to see us not long after our arrival on Crete. They had located their own unit through the transit camp near Chania and eventually their unit camped quite close to us. Unfortunately they were both killed later in the fight to try and hold the Maleme airport.

Crete was occupied by the British at the request of the Greek Government in November 1940 in order to prevent Italian seizure. It was not heavily fortified as apparently the idea was to beat the Italians in Africa and hold the mainland in Greece.

Much of the equipment and small arms was lost in transit between Greece and Crete. Although the troops in Greece were in bad shape when they first arrived on Crete we got about three weeks respite before the real blitz began. The troops had picked up well but for many units, ours included, there were no weapons available. D Company were not with us on the *Costa Rica* and had landed safely with their full compliment of twelve Vickers 303 guns and they remained through the show; the remainder of us being evacuated before any earnest fighting took place.

After being informed that large concentrations of troop planes were observed in Greece and that an airborne attack on Crete was imminent, it fell the lot of the rebel section attaching a white singlet to a stick in the fashion of a flag and signal Morse code between patrols and down to HQ at the foot of the steep hill. Horrie played a very important part here during the night. Having no signalling lamps or even torches, communications at night had to be effected by runner, and as it was particularly steep between HQ and the nearest patrol it was a slow job for the runner to scramble down to HQ with any message.

During the day Horrie and I remained with the patrol that occupied the position nearest to HQ. Just before dark I would return to HQ leaving Horrie tied up and remaining with the patrol.

If the patrol received any message by runner to be forwarded to HQ it was wrapped securely in a handkerchief and tied to Horrie's collar, he would then be released and needed no instruction to find me below. He would come straight to the hollow olive tree where I slept and a lick of affection on my face always woke me to receive the message, the receipt was acknowledged by Poppa firing two rapid shots into the air with his revolver.

Although no enemy action was experienced by the patrols, Horrie was used on five or six occasions and he did not fail on any occasion; he could negotiate the distance in the dark in less than a quarter of the time it would take a runner to do the same distance.

We were evacuated from Crete on the *Lossiebank* and it was on this ship that Horrie was hit by a small piece of shrapnel, or rather a bomb splinter. On our arrival at Dier Suneid we moved into a prepared area; tents etc were already set up to receive us.

We were met by the Gogg and Big Jim, they escorted us to a tent where we found a fair quantity of Australian beer that they had secured to welcome us back. Horrie recognised his two old friends immediately and was as excited as they were. After shaking hands all round, Big Jim asked to be excused for a few minutes, taking Horrie with him he disappeared. When they returned back at the tent a few minutes later, Big Jim opened a paper parcel he was carrying and Horrie was offered a dog's dream in the way of cooked meat. "Officers Mess?" enquired Poppa. Big Jim only laughed. We guessed someone would be a bit 'light on' (not enough) in the Officer's Mess that day.

"Lost quite a lot of weight but looks lively enough," remarked Big Jim looking at Horrie who was very busy. "He has grown quite a lot," observed the Gogg, opening a bottle. Between drinks, tales of Horrie were told. Big Jim and the Gogg were all attention and Horrie often hearing his name mentioned sat in the centre of the tent watching our faces closely. "So Horrie is a little Anzac," laughed Big Jim.

As though in reply, Horrie took up position of guard at the door of the tent. "Wogs," said the Gogg. Horrie stood alert and growled. "Wouldn't that rip yer!" remarked Murchie. Horrie, after a good feed was prepared to 'soldier on' immediately.

It was a happy reunion and lasted far into the night when Poppa and Big Jim retired, Big Jim advised "Reveille at 0600hrs." "Like hell!" we all replied. Big Jim laughed "Goodnight you Rebels" "Lets drink a toast," suggested Murchie. "Okay," we replied. "To those who gave their all…" Soberly we drank the toast. During the next few days dozens of soldiers from various units called to see Horrie. They had been told about him from their friends whom they had called to see in our unit; the little wog dog posed for dozens of cameras.

They were lazy days our first few in Palestine, we were given plenty of rest and extra good food. Horrie quickly picked up his lost weight and he spent many hours chasing his old friends the lizards just for fun. Arab natives also received his earnest attention, routine orders said no natives allowed in the camp area and Horrie carried out the orders very thoroughly.

The natives in the Dier Suneid area were notorious thieves and rifles had to be chained to the tent pole during the night, in spite of close watch by prowling piquets, it became necessary for a lamp to remain burning in the tent all night and the occupants to take it in turns to remain awake in the tent. We lost nothing at all in our tent, not even sleep, thanks to Horrie.

Route marches commenced again, troops must harden up and get fit, these were indeed happy days for the little wog dog. The village of Dier Suneid was about half a mile from our camp and as it was placed out of bounds to the troops it appeared more interesting than it actually was.

Don, Feathers and myself, unable to resist the temptation any longer, decided to see for ourselves what dark and sinister mysteries it held. Poppa who had been in the area during the 1914-1918 war, wetted our appetite by painting wild pictures of dusky damsels dressed in shimmering veils dancing to the weird wailing native music. Feathers got hold of a book on Arabic, and leaving Horrie tied to the tent pole we set out for the glorious adventure. Fortunately Horrie came to our rescue and we were able to make a less undignified exit.

We approached the village through an orange grove that screened the village from the main Tel-Aviv-Gaza road. A high mud and straw wall surrounded the village and the only opening appeared directly in front of us. When we emerged from the orange grove through the opening we could see a narrow winding street lined each side by a wall, openings in the shape of archways led into separate yards in front of the actual dwellings.

It seemed peaceful enough, small urchins played in the street, fowls and donkeys roamed at random in and out of the archways. We walked slowly up the street the subject of interest to the urchins and villagers as we passed. "Looks like a few soldiers have been here," I remarked. We had by this time a considerable following, the natives must have been familiar with the sight of Australian soldiers.

An elderly native astride a small donkey passed us moving in the opposite direction. Feathers made a noise like a cross between a hiccup, a snore and a knife being scraped on the edge of a tin plate but the elderly Arab passed by unheedingly. "What the hell did you say?"I enquired. Feathers consulted his book again and replied, "I wished him that Allah smile upon him and his family, and may all his chickens be hens." Don and I laughed. "Looks like, by his attitude, that all his chickens are roosters," replied Don. "Do you think it possible he did not understand your Arabic?" I asked Feathers. "No chance of that," replied Feathers, quite indignant. The urchins who had followed us up the street had overcome their curiosity and were now asking for Bak-sheesh, turning to them we threw a few mils and while they scrambled on the ground we continued along the street.

The smell of the village was overpowering and Feathers remarked that the alluring exotic perfume that the dark beauties were supposed to use would have an uphill job to smother the odours of the village. "It's on the bugle (nose) alright," replied Don, while I considered it bad enough to stop your watch. The urchins had caught up with us again and we parted with another handful of coins, this last contribution left us flat broke.

A very unpleasant looking individual stopped us as we drew abreast of the doorway where he was standing. "Can Can," he said and beckoned us to follow him to the dwelling at the rear of the little yard. "What do you say?" Feathers enquired of us. Don and I, who had seen this performance in Egypt, had no desire to witness it again and the Arab apparently noticed our hesitation, "Cognac, very clean Cognac," he enquired, thinking it may be a better idea if we drank a bottle of Wog Cognac first. "Finish money George," I replied. "Cognac good!" he replied, "500 mils, Australia plenty money." "Finish money," I replied again getting a little annoyed.

The urchins who once again had crowded around us overheard my remark, our money finished they withdrew a little and replaced the sugar with vinegar. Cat calls and stones started to fly in our direction. I noticed a few tough looking natives kept beefing the urchins and were scowling at us and urging the urchins on. The situation looked unpleasant, as the urchins were between us and the exit from the village, we could scarcely knock the kids about and it looked like we would have to take it all on the way out. "I'd like to get at that big black sod urging the urchins on over there," remarked Feathers. "Looks like Wogs day out," replied Don. "Baksheesh bukra (tomorrow)," I called in a last effort to quieten the kids but a further shower of stones was the reply.

At this moment squeals and shrieks announced the arrival of Horrie at the entrance to the village, his familiar bark rising above the din. Horrie cleared the street in no time. Sighting us only put more enthusiasm into the pup and he refused to hear me call him, however we started to run and calling Horrie, I picked him up and we gracefully walked out. "He saved our dignity a little," laughed Feathers. "Guess it was our own fault for barging into the village anyway," I replied.

On the way back to camp we decided not to tell the Rebels about the adventure. Horrie apparently kept thinking about the incident as he would growl and pop out the tent more often than usual that night. "What's up with Horrie tonight I wonder?" enquired Fitz. "Wogs," replied Gordie. Don, Feathers and I laughed. Later that night when Poppa dropped by for his usual cup of tea I asked him if he had ever tried the Wog Cognac. "Only once during the last stoush," he replied, "And I was overwhelmed by little blue mice. A pink elephant saved me in the nick of time by trampling them to death."

The entire rebel section including Poppa and Horrie visited Jerusalem. Jerusalem proved a striking contrast of the modern city and the old. The little guide we adopted for the day (the son of Sandy McKenzie) took us through the market place or bazaar. It was almost like an underground city.

The narrow streets were covered over after the style of an arcade, its only light supplied by oblong openings in the roof. These openings measured some 2ft by 6ft long and were about 15ft apart; the light murkiness of the interior.

The windows of small jewellery shops lit from inside by lamps reflected light that gleamed in the darkness. Here and there open butcher shops displayed tables of chopped up meat exposed to the street and myriads of flies, while fruit and vegetable stalls extended across the footpath and onto the road. Numerous little donkeys passing to and fro often laden with goods that appeared twice the size of the donkey itself; on top of the load sat the 'Lord and Master' while struggling behind also loaded with goods his wife and family.

Black clad Arab women peered over cloaks drawn up just under their eyes, strings of silver coins hung down from their hooded headdress and covered the nose. The babble of strange voices haggled over prices without which a sale is never effected. Coloured flags drooped dejected looking over dwellings. A white flag advertised the fact that therein lived a marriageable daughter, blue for an unmarried mother with child, black for a widow whose marriage her father was willing to pay a dowry. Green meant that the occupant was away on a pilgrimage to Mecca.

It was a picture of the East unchanged since the time of Christ, all this contrasted with the modern Jerusalem. To pass from the ancient city to the new was like awakening after a thousand years of sleep. Modern buildings lined clean wide concrete roads along which numerous taxis scooted about driven by Arab drivers who placed their entire faith in Allah and good brakes; the traffic directed by tall Englishmen clothed in the blue uniform and white helmet of the Palestinian Police Force. Modern picture theatres. During the film, French, Arabic and Hebrew was flashed on a strip alongside the screen to enable those unable to understand English to follow the picture.

Generously wide white concrete footpaths reflected a light so glaring that ninety percent of the people wore sunglasses. Wide front modern shops displayed glittering jewellery and all the vivid and gorgeous silks of the East. The soberly dark gowns of priests of countless religions mingled with the bright flimsy frocks and sporty gay coloured shorts. Large open Cafés with the tables and chairs extending on to the footpath, protected from the sun by gaily coloured veranda blinds, reminiscent of Paris. The grey slacks and light open necked shirts of the men gave the modern city a carefree atmosphere.

When it became apparent we were to miss the campaign in Syria, mainly due to the loss of equipment not yet replaced after the Greece and Crete show, Murchie became very restless. "The 2/3rd Machine Gunners look like being in it, what about getting a transfer over to their unit?" he asked. The rebel section talked this over but the problem that confronted us was Horrie. "Horrie may not be accepted as part of their show like he is here?" I queried. "We could not go anywhere without him now," replied Don. Horrie sat on my bed and listened carefully. "That little bloke knows every word we say!" remarked Poppa patting the little wog dog. It seemed so: 'Don't leave me behind' his expression pleaded.

Murchie decided to transfer to the 2/3rd M/G Btn and after the show in Syria try and rejoin us again. We were sorry to see him go. I remember his last words very clearly: "Good luck you chaps and good luck little wog dog." Horrie knew he was losing a good friend also, he stood on his hind legs and rested his front paws on Murchie's knee as Murchie knelt down to pat him. Long after Murchie was out of sight Horrie sat outside the tent looking in the direction Murchie had taken. We never saw Murchie again. He is somewhere in Java, but our guess is he is back in the hills somewhere still holding out, who could imagine Murchie an unwilling guest of the 'yellow warts'.

Some short time later I was sent to a School of Signals at Dimeria about two miles from our camp at Dier Suneid. Horrie and Don walked across to my temporary camp, Don giving me a hand to carry my gear. After I had settled in Don and Horrie returned to Dier Suneid.

Just before midday the following day I was listening to a lecture on the mysteries of choke-coils and transformers, etc given by Sgt Bell. "Hello, where did you come from?" These words from Bell made me look up from the notes I was taking down and there larger than life was the little wog dog.

"Horrie," I called, with a yelp of excitement he scrambled under legs to reach me. I picked him up and his little elongated body wriggled and squirmed in pleasure. I explained to Sgt Bell that Horrie was the signal platoon mascot of my unit and the wog dog was permitted to stay in the lecture room until the midday break.

During the lunch hour Horrie and I walked back to our camp at Dier Suneid, the wog dog very pleased with his efforts to find me showed his pleasure with numerous wags of his tail.

Returning to the Rebels tent I found it empty. Leaving Horrie tied to the tent pole I sought out Big Jim and enquired where the Rebels were to be found. "They are fanned out all over Palestine looking for Horrie," he explained. Poor Horrie had to be tied up to the tent for the next three weeks to prevent him attending lectures on signal duties. 'Communications must go through.' The lecture under this heading took me back to Crete and the little dog playing his part, I was still in Crete when the lecture ended. Returning to my unit and the Rebels I was to find myself well on the way towards becoming a Field Marshall.

"Lance Corporal is your new title," advised Big Jim.

That night I took a considerable ragging in the Rebels tent.

"Please may we smoke sir?" from Fitz. "Guess your old man will move to a bigger house and stop talking to the neighbours," remarked Don. "What about writing a book on how you rose from the ranks?" asked Gordie.

I evacuated the tent and sought out Poppa, between us we worked out a scheme. Later when I entered the tent the Rebels sprang to attention. "Carry on," I advised them, "I was a private myself once."

Poppa entered later and in a serious voice said to me "Corporal I want three men for a special piquet." "Don, Fitz and Gordie," I replied. "Gogg you put on a brew of tea for Poppa, Feathers and myself, after that you may take Horrie for a walk." "Are you fair dinkum?" inquired Fitz. "Please refrain from using slang in the presence of your superiors," I replied. I went down struggling and while pinned helplessly to the ground Horrie licked my face just to show there was no animosity.

We moved from our camp at Dier Suneid to Khassa. The area we occupied at Khassa was alongside the 2/1st Anti-Tank Regiment, just arrived back in Palestine after the Syria show. After we had settled in I strolled over to the Anti-Tank lines to locate an old friend, Bruce McKellar. Horrie trotted at my side. Entering the camp lines a soldier called "Imshee" (buzz off) to me. "What's biting you?" I replied taken aback at this reception. "It's okay Dig, don't get your wool off," he laughed as Horrie and I strode over to him, "I thought it was our little dog Imshee," he informed me.

I laughed and told him that this was the Machine Gunners' dog Horrie. Imshee he informed me had been with the Anti-Tank Regiment in Egypt, Greece and Syria. I replied that Horrie had not yet been in Syria but he was on a troopship that was bombed and sunk. "Guess that about evens things up," he laughed.

Finding Mac I later asked him about Imshee. He told me that the little dog was the pet of one of their cooks and that the cook devoted more interest in preparing a meal for his little dog than he did for the troops. "She would probably appreciate it more anyway," I laughed. While Mac and I were talking, Horrie wandered off around the camp. Calling him he came trotting back accompanied by Imshee. Very pleased with himself he introduced me to Imshee. I bent down and called her to me, she came to me but appeared a little timid. Horrie fussed about me and informed her everything was alright as I was a cobber of his.

Imshee seemed to be the same breed as Horrie, her colouring was exactly the same but she stood about two inches higher than Horrie and was not quite so deep in the chest, her tail was a little longer also. While Mac and I stood watching them, Imshee was plainly trying to capture the wog dog's heart. Pretending to take no notice of Horrie she proudly pranced about holding her neck very high, often she would disappear behind a tent only to reappear soon after as Horrie had not followed her. "Go on Horrie," I said. As Horrie trotted over to her she sat down and appeared to be interested in the horizon.

Horrie gave an enquiring sniff at her face but Imshee turned her head away, Horrie playfully took hold of her ear and pulled. Imshee very annoyed at the loss of her dignity snapped and Horrie backed off a little way and viewed her with his head on one side. "No ordinary street pick up this lass," I remarked to Mac. Horrie unable to fathom Imshee's attitude trotted back to me for advice. Imshee gave a yelp and raced off after some mythical object in the distance, Horrie needed no advice now and excitedly raced after her. "Horrie is gradually making up ground," I informed Mac. "Reckon Imshee isn't trying!" laughed Mac, as we watched the two little white objects gradually disappear across the sandy waste.

It was late that night when Horrie climbed onto the foot of my bed. "Imshee's a nice little dog," I said to him and I could feel his little tail moving at my feet in agreement. As the days passed Horrie and Imshee became inseparable. Horrie was then torn between his desire to accompany us on route marches and to remain with Imshee. He tried hard to get Imshee to accompany us also but she would never move far from the camp area. Horrie would stop with her until we were a long way off then telling her 'he would see her tonight' he would come scampering after us. Catching up he would take his place alongside Big Jim; 'after all soldiering must come before pleasure,' but he would look back at us now and again with a wide grin for being late. "You are a dinkum rebel alright," Jim would scold him.

'I'm one of the boys,' Horrie would grin.

The L.A.D (Light Aid Detachment) attached to our unit had adopted a huge Alsatian that had wandered into the camp, and as he had arrived in this area they called him Khassa. Khassa was an excellent watchdog but he was inclined to be treacherous and sulky. Horrie had warned him not to come too close to our tent, it looked so funny to see little Horrie growl in no uncertain manner at Khassa when he came near our tent. Watching Horrie growl at this huge dog one day, Don exclaimed that we should rename Horrie 'steak', because he was so tough.

The Gogg reckoned Horrie was bluffing, but it was certainly no bluff. Imshee was on her way over to visit Horrie when she was waylaid by Khassa not far from our tent. Imshee's yelp for help reached Horrie who was dozing at the foot of my bed. Like a bolt from the blue he was out of the tent and seeing his girlfriend in distress, he made straight for Khassa. Khassa turned his attention from the cornered Imshee to that of the insignificant wog dog.

Frank Bruce, our R.A.P Cpl noticed the incident and fearing Horrie would be seriously hurt raced after him. Without hesitating Horrrie flew straight at Khassa, Imshee backed away to a safe distance to watch the gallant Horrie. Horrie adopted the only tactic that had a reasonable chance of success from such a small attacking force, the speed of his attack completely upset the large dog and before Khassa had time to regain, Horrie had secured a painful hold on Khassa's hind paw. The big dog yelped and snarled in pain but Horrie dragged the hind leg round and round, at the same time being able to keep out of reach of the snapping fangs. Imshee seeing Khassa fall joined in, as Khassa twisted his head and neck around to snap at Horrie, Imshee would dart in, secure Khassa by the back of the neck and drag his head back then nimbly jump back out of reach; it was perfect coordination and Khassa was completely outwitted.

Frank Bruce tried to separate the brawling dogs and although he was able to break it up before the powerful Khassa could turn the tables, he received a bad gash on the arm that later required several stitches. Snarling in pain Khassa limped away while Horrie advanced a few paces in front of Imshee and growled his warning to Khassa to keep moving. After receiving a pat of praise from Frank he proudly escorted Imshee back to the Anti-Tank lines. Poor Frank had a painful reminder of the scrap for quite a few days. Later that night when he told us of the incident we praised Horrie: 'some scrapping dog, our wog dog.'

The day arrived for the Anti-Tank to move back again to Syria and Horrie was left to fret for awhile over Imshee's absence. News of the cold conditions in Syria drifted back to us in Palestine and as we expected to move to Syria, we were issued with woollen gloves, bala-clavas and scarves, a gift from the Australian Comforts Fund. "How do you think Horrie will take to the snow?" enquired Feathers. It was this remark that gave birth to the idea of a uniform for Horrie.

Don produced an old greatcoat that he scrounged from a salvage dump and together Don and I started on the tedious task of making Horrie a coat. Suggestions both helpful and otherwise were made by the Rebels during the fitting. First of all the tail of the coat was cut off, and after standing Horrie up on my bed we draped the piece of coat over him. Horrie stood quite still but he appeared a little dubious. Having found the required length I snipped off the unrequired material of the stern end. "Careful of his rudder," advised the Gogg, as though he understood, Horrie sat down for safety.

Next we measured the width between his two front legs and cut holes accordingly in the front end of the cloth. Placing the cloth over him again we put his front legs through the holes then snipped the unrequired cloth under his chest and belly, leaving just enough to fasten with buttons.

At the stern end we snipped the cloth away leaving one long strip each side, these came down over his rump each side of the tail then under the leg and back again to fasten on the side, making two loops at the rear of his legs. Gordie remarked that it would not be necessary to wrap his tail up as it might spoil his carriage. Fitz replied, "I don't know about his carriage but it would ruin his wagging."

However we overcame the difficulty by cutting a half moon in the cloth around Horrie's rudder. Telling Horrie that he was a good dog, I proved to Fitz there was nothing of matter with the wagging.

The places for buttons and button holes were marked with a piece of chalk and we attached the unit colour patch to the top of the neck piece. I engaged Feather's attention to the excellent features of the uniform while Don cut the buttons off Feather's tunic that was hanging on the tent pole.

We trimmed the edges of the uniform with tape, attached the buttons and finished the outfit off by attaching two little gold stripes to the tunic over the right leg. The uniform fitted very well and did not hamper his movements in any way. Horrie was very proud of it in spite of the amusement of the mob.

Receiving a mouth organ in a parcel from home I endeavoured to brighten the Rebels camp with music, but as I had to pass through the beginners stage it was not appreciated by anyone except Horrie.

"Can you play far far away?" enquired Don. "I'll give it a fly," I answered quite bucked at this unexpected encouragement "Well that's the direction!" he said, pointing to the vast empty stretch of desert.

Fitz suggested that I should train Horrie to sit up and hold my hat in his mouth. The Gogg offered to paint a sign 'spare a coin for an old digger' and suggested I could hang it around my neck. But the faithful wog dog stuck by me and he would voice his accompaniment with much gusto. "Horrie appreciates music anyway," I told the Rebels but they reckoned Horrie was expressing his agony much better than they could.

Leave was plentiful just prior to our move up to Syria, but as it was on a percentage basis per platoon, it was seldom that more than two of the Rebels could go on leave together. As Horrie took such a good view of going on leave, whoever was granted leave among the rebel section always took Horrie along with them. It was not looked upon by the Rebels as anything unusual to take the little dog on leave with them, but rather the accepted thing. Consequently Horrie had numerous trips to several places in Palestine. As the unusual sight of a little dog wearing a uniform attracted the attention of many it was not long before soldiers and strangers got to know him by name. 'Hello Horrie.' 'That's the little wog dog,' etc was often heard. Soldiers clubs, popular Cafés, dance halls, beaches etc; wherever soldiers went on leave Horrie went also.

If the Rebels called in for a drink at any of the numerous wine and spirit Cafés, Horrie accompanied them. He would be sat up upon the counters and given a saucer of milk. Horrie, who considered himself one of the boys, would accept the refreshment with much tail wagging, no matter how many calls of this nature were made; Horrie would never let it be said he couldn't take it and often the little dog would be blown out like barrage balloon.

The Jewish and Arab Café owners often tried to pat him but they received no uncertain warning that his only accepted friends were all wearing the A.I.F uniform; he was a Digger's dog.

A few days before our move up to Syria Big Jim popped into the tent. "Will you have Horrie here at 2pm," he asked, "As a most unexpected visitor wishes to see him." "Who is it?" I asked. "You will find out at 2pm, but be prepared for a shock," he replied. At 2pm who should arrive but Captain J. Hindmarsh.

Prior to this we believed him to be a guest of the Nazis in Greece but by some means he had escaped and caught up with us in Palestine. Horrie recognised him immediately and was as pleased as we were. "I had often wondered about the little dog and whether you still had him," he remarked. Capt. Hindmarsh was to take over our company as OC.

Horrie's luck was holding out as his old friend Capt. Plummers was to be replaced with another friendly OC.

The natives we encountered in Syria were undoubtedly good sports. Many of them remembered the old diggers from the 1914-1918 war, although not many could speak English they could all say 'Heads and Tails' and know the difference. They were very keen 'two-up' players and the boys called them 'grouter betters'. This term was used to describe betters who would wait until three or four heads or tails fell in succession before placing their bet; putting their faith in the law of averages that the next fall of pennies was likely to turn the opposite to that of the succession.

Often when the troops and natives were unable to agree on the price of some small souvenir, the natives would say 'Toss'; they called their fancy and if they won their price was paid, if not the soldier secured his souvenir at his price. I rather fancy they knew the game of 'two-up' before we arrived and they were very lucky. Several times I noticed little groups of natives playing among themselves.

At the time Horrie was sick in Syria it was bitterly cold, although not snowing an icy wind blew up along the valley. The inside of our tin hut was heated by a small wood heater placed in the centre of the hut. This to some extent afforded the hut with some warmth. As the many callers inquiring after Horrie would invariably be accompanied by an icy cold blast as they opened the door, the small wood burners had an uphill job to keep the hut warm.

We had placed Horrie's box as near to the burner as possible, but in spite of this and the warm rocks in his bed he would shiver visibly when the wind blew into the hut. Poppa conceived the idea of the bulletin after being told to quickly close the B- door after him. Poppa suggested that if we posted a bulletin on the outside of the door we would be able to keep the hut warm and at the same time inform the many inquirers as to Horrie's condition.

The Gogg was given the job of printing the bulletin. A large notice was printed on a piece of cardboard and tacked above the bulletin, 'DON'T OPEN THIS DOOR'. The bulletin was posted up twice daily and read as follows: 'This door when opened admits a cold wind which lessens our chance of keeping the wog dog warm, the condition of Horrie continues to be grave, he answers to his name only by opening his eyes. He accepted only a little warm porridge during the morning, everything possible is being done to keep him warm, so don't muck it up by opening the door. A further bulletin will be issued at 1700 hrs. (5pm).' After the arrival of Imshee a special bulletin was issued: 'The wog dogs girlfriend Imshee is now at his bedside, don't panic, the services of the Padre will not be required, Horrie showed a new interest in life after a visit from his girlfriend.'

When the first Australian. Anti-Tank Reg. arrived my old friend Bruce MacKellar sought me out and found me on duty in a tin shed that served as our Signal Office. "How's the wog dog?" he enquired. "Not so good, he seems to have a severe chill," I replied. "Did Imshee come to this camp with you?" I enquired. "The section she is with should be here anytime now," he replied.

Thinking that Imshee may arouse a little interest in Horrie I asked Mac to bring her over when she arrived. It was about midday when Mac came over with Imshee under his arm. Imshee also wore a uniform, not quite so elaborate as Horrie's but it was comfortable and warm.

Mac and I walked up from the Signal Office to my hut and arriving found the Rebels and several more Sigs. clustered around the heater, Horrie was asleep in his box. "Horrie look who's here!" I called to him as Mac put Imshee down alongside his box. Imshee sniffed inquiringly at Horrie. Horrie 'certainly' came to life, suddenly he scrambled out of his box full of beans, his little tail wagging for all its worth.

Surprise registered on all the faces of the mob. "You B- little malingerer!" laughed Gordie. Horrie was called some unprintable kinds of a scoundrel, but he was far too pleased at meeting Imshee again to take any notice.

They examined each other's uniforms with such obvious approval that it was comical to watch. "Horrie!" I called, "Bed's the best place for sick little wog dogs," and picking him up I put him back in his box; "And what's more, stop there and don't dare to get out!" "That will teach you to put the old soldier act over us," Don told him. Horrie propped his chin over the edge of the box and looked very dejected.

I was the first up the following morning and when I opened the door Imshee was waiting there for Horrie, I let her enter the hut and she trotted over to Horrie's box. Horrie looked at me very pleadingly : 'Can I go out ?' "Off you go rascal" was sufficient to send Horrie and his girlfriend to the door and they trotted away together to investigate the bushes around the camp.

Horrie found out for himself that if the door of the hut was shut he had only to bark and one of the Sigs. would open it for him. On this occasion his familiar bark sent Fitz to the door, Horrie and Imshee popped in. They were covered from head to tail in red mud. Looking very pleased with themselves they joined the Sigs. at the heater, as their little uniforms were wet the boys removed them and hung them up near the heater to dry. "You little grub," Feathers remarked as he scraped some of the mud off with a piece of stick. Horrie accepted this as praise and grinned. Don was trying to scrape mud off Imshee also when her master's voice floated across to us. Imshee always very obedient trotted over to the door, I followed to open it up for her, Feathers held Horrie to prevent him from following her; "You stop here until you get dry," he told Horrie.

As Imshee raced across to her master, Don remarked "What about her coat?" "Let Horrie take it to her," advised the Gogg. He took the coat down from the drying rack and handed it to me. "Take Imshee's coat to her," I told him and he understood immediately. Very proudly he trotted after Imshee and her master, holding the coat in his mouth.

"Hold on a bit, Imshee's coat!" Don called to Imshee's master. Imshee and her boss stopped and turned around, Imshee trotted back to meet Horrie, but instead of dropping her coat he invited her to play.

Just keeping out of reach of Imshee's boss he dodged and turned and scooted round with Imshee following him, gradually working his way back to the laughing Sigs at the doorway of our hut, suddenly he made straight for the door with Imshee following.

We parted to let them out but Horrie made straight for the heater then dropping the coat sat down, Imshee stood watching him for a moment then sat down alongside him "The cunning little blighter has kidded her back again," observed Gordie, and no doubt that was the little wog dogs idea. We laughingly explained the wog dog's scheme to Imshee's master. "I know," he replied,"The little so and so spends half his time kidding her away from our camp!" but Imshee was permitted to stay for awhile.

Africans were recruited as a labour battalion, their Officers, Tommies, but they supplied their own NCO's. Of exceptionally fine physique they measured up to 6 feet, built in proportion to their height, jet black, large squat noses and fine white teeth. Very jovial and cheery, always laughing and joking among themselves. They were well wrapped up in woollen scarves and balaclavas and dressed in the Tommy regulation battle dress. Unable to speak much English and there is some doubt about the place they came from, some say 'Evacualand', others 'Bechuanaland'.

At the time Horrie Don and I encountered them they were digging a tank trap across the Lebanese valley. The incident relating to their donning gas masks when it started to snow is hearsay, many whom I have approached remember the incident but were unable to name anyone who actually saw it.

They were working on the trap about three miles north of our gun position. I recall that quite a few boys remarked on their cheerfulness as they must have been more out of their natural element in this climate than we were, and the cold worried us a bit.

When Horrie sighted them and decided to capture the lot they ran up and down the sides of the trap, some laughingly climbed on their friends backs in an effort to escape Horrie who had a set plan in mind. He endeavoured to get them all down in the tank trap. He would concentrate on one until he had run down the slope, then barking and yelping he would return up again and attack another until he achieved his purpose. Fortunately these cheery coves thought it a huge joke and they thoroughly enjoyed the game, seeing that they were enjoying it so much we let Horrie rip and eventually he got them all down at the bottom of the trap or up on the opposite bank.

They kept him busy as one would attract his attention by calling and climbing up our side while another would sneak up quietly further down. Up and down along the bank on our side scooted Horrie determined that none should get up our side, exhausted he returned to us and I picked the panting pup up. The Africans came across to us and the more adventurous extended a hand to pat Horrie, however a growl and showing of his teeth greeted the venturous hand, and it was quickly withdrawn to the accompaniment of much laughter from their friends. The fact that they laughed at him made Horrie furious but it was great fun for the Africans.

The Lebanese mountains that rose up each side of our camp at Zaboude in the valley, rose approximately 3000 ft. The day Horrie accompanied Don and I we climbed the rise on the eastern side of the valley. Exceptionally steep and rocky and in many places unscaleable, there were very few trees, for most part the vegetation was a scrub resembling Holly. The mountain was deceiving from the valley below as it appeared to be one gradual slope to the summit, however once up the first 1000 ft it presented a very different sight. Numerous little false crests and small valleys appeared between us and the top.

It was in these small valleys on the mountainside that the Lebanese villages nestled, mostly they comprised of only two or three dwellings of mud and rock structure. The roofs were quite flat, on each roof there was a small stone roller about the size of an ordinary home lawn mower, apparently these rollers were used to roll the roof and so keep it flat and compressed. The outlet above the fireplace extended above the roof to the height of only about 18 inches. In quite a few cases the hillside had been cut away sheer to form one of the four sides of the dwelling.

The villagers we contacted were Christian Arabs and proud of the fact, although the men folk wore the traditional Arab dress, sheep-skin coats and long wide pantaloons caught in tight below the knees and very baggy between the legs. The women folk wore tattered remnants of European dresses, they were very friendly and on contacting them they would immediately beckon you inside and proudly point to pictures of Christ and the Virgin Mary that were the only ornaments inside the dwellings.

These villagers were very poor, their entire existence depended upon their small flocks of goats and sheep and tiny cultivated fields of wheat. The wheat was pounded in an earthenware dish by round tapered rocks, the result was baked into bread shaped like a flat pancake, this, olives and sour cheese made from goats milk comprised their main diet. Very few could speak English but almost all could speak French, probably due to the French influence in Syria since the last war.

The British Government had relieved the serious food shortage in Syria after the collapse of the Vichy French but even these villagers barely existed. They were very proud these Christian Arabs and unlike the Muslim Arabs they would never ask for Baksheesh. Distrustful also of the Muslims, they would warn us: Muslim 'Klefti' (steal) They liked the French which surprised us a little as they were in a very bad position regarding any help in the food shortage until the British took over Syria. Turkey they were also mistrustful of. Turkey

Muslim 'Musquise' (no good) they informed us.

Corrales were built of rocks close to the villages, here their small flocks were herded at night to protect them from the cold and the wolves that roamed the hills at night. Each village possessed several huge dogs similar to the Alsatian, only more wolf-looking. In every case we noticed that the tips of the ears were missing on the huge beasts and this was probably due to frost bite. Lean and scraggy, they were ferocious to strangers (us) but obedient to their owner, who hearing the beasts snarl at us would call them off and make them stay inside the dwellings until we had passed.

Returning to camp we were greeted by Imshee. She barked her greetings to Horrie who went ahead to meet her, no doubt to tell her how he cleaned the wolf up. Leaving the two dogs playing, Don and I dropped into the Signal Office. Fitz, Gordie, Feathers and Poppa were in the Signal hut. "About time you two showed up," declared Poppa, "Have you heard the news?" "What news?" I asked. "Yesterday the Japs attacked Pearl Harbour from the air," replied Poppa "Don't know the extent of the damage as yet but you can bet your sweet life it will be popping in the Pacific now," he continued. "I suppose the Yanks will declare the Axis on as well?" enquired Feathers. We all agreed that we thought it a certainty. "It might wake them up a bit here," declared Gordie. "What difference do you think the Japs attack will have on us?" I asked Poppa. "I don't see that it will make much difference to us," he replied. "Britain will probably declare the Japs on, and with the Yankee Pacific fleet and our stronghold on Singapore I don't think that we will be needed back home, and don't forget there is plenty to be done in this part of the globe," he continued. The rest of the Rebels were not so sure.

"It does not look so good to my way of thinking, surely the Japs are not stupid enough to start something that they think they have no hope of finishing?" I replied. "Anyway at least we know how we stand with the Japs now," remarked Don. "The Yanks will give them a bit for their corner," remarked Fitz. "I'll bet the Woman's Weekly boys are excited, they look like getting a scrap after all," remarked Gordie. (The name 'woman's weekly boys' was given jokingly to the 8th Division by the troops in the Middle East, the reason being that every time we picked the Woman's Weekly up we read of our troops in Malaya) "I'd like to be with them now," from Feathers. "Me too," replied Don, "It would be better than freezing to death doing nothing here."

Pearl Harbour was the topic of the camp, most of the troops were astounded that the Japanese had the cheek to attack such a power as the U.S.A, many were glad that at last the Japs had declared their hand and the danger in the Pacific would be quickly removed once and for all by the Yanks.

I received a letter from an old pal Happy McMillan, his unit the 2/2nd Hwy AA Reg. were camped at Tripoli (Syria) which by the inland route through Homs was about 100 miles from our camp at Zaboude. "I'd like to get up and see Happy," I remarked to Do, "But there is no chance of getting leave unfortunately." Later when I was talking to Mac at the Anti-Tank camp I happened to mention my desire to get up to Tripoli. "We've got a truck going up there at 5.30 in the morning and returning the same day," he informed me, "Guess we can fit you in if you can manage to get away for the day."

I arranged with Don to do his shift on the switch board during the night and he was to take my place during the next day, so the following morning Horrie and I set off for Tripoli. The back of the truck was open and as it was bitterly cold, Horrie and I curled up in one corner and being tired from loss of sleep during the night, I slept until we arrived at Tripoli some five hours later.

Making arrangements to pick the truck up at 6pm that night, Horrie and I, frozen to the bone, stiffly hobbled off to try and locate Happy's gun section. Eventually finding his section Happy tried to thaw me out with rum with an 'H'. This rum was spelt Rhum and called rum with an 'H' by the troops. It was of very doubtful origin and had a wallop like an army mule. Horrie was well known to Happy's pack and hearing he was in their camp numerous lads arrived to see Horrie and he accepted their attention while I received the Rhum. I very soon thawed out and as Happy warmed up also he suggested that we 'do Tripoli over'. Horrie, Happy and myself set out for the Soldiers Club in the town. Arriving there we found both the service and the beer excellent. Consequently Tripoli remained standing but Horrie and I only just missed the returning truck by fifteen hours.

Arising at 9am the next morning I fought my way to my feet, steadied the tent with one hand and looked about for Happy. I found him asleep curled up alongside his bed. I had slept on one side, Happy on the other and in the middle Horrie.

After Horrie had his breakfast I bid Happy goodbye and with a head like a statue I set a course in a southerly direction. Horrie and I managed to get a lift and we eventually got back to Zaboude at 4pm. As we reached the camp, Horrie hopped off to find Imshee and I made my way to the Signal Office. Entering I found the Rebels sitting around the heater. "Is there a Doctor in the house?" I enquired. They looked around and laughed. "You don't need a Doctor, what you need is a Lawyer!" laughed Fitz. "Did you bring any grog back with you?" inquired the Gogg. "Yes," I replied, "That's why I need a Doctor."

Horrie who had apparently been unable to find Imshee, came wagging his way in. "Did I get shot down?" I asked (caught). "The General died at dawn..." replied Don mournfully, the Rebels hung their heads. "Finish Lance Corporal," sobbed Fitz. "Finish Corporal Horrie too!" laughed the Gogg. Horrie hearing his name wagged his tail and grinned. "Wipe that grin off your face Cpl Horrie," said the Gogg. "So you think you can beat the rap," Don said to Horrie. "Wait a minute you blokes, Horrie should not lose his stripes as he was not responsible for being AWL," I declared.

"Nevertheless he was Ack Willie (AWL)," insisted the Gogg. "Well, out of fairness to Horrie I suggest he at least be given a trial, that is if I get tossed (lose the verdict)," I replied. "Well the position is this," disclosed Fitz "If you get shot down by the old man (CO), Horrie will be tried for being AWL also; if you beat the rap Horrie gets off also." "Ok that's fair enough," I laughed. The next night at Horrie's trial, Poppa was asked to take the place of the CO, Feathers was to be the Adjutant, Don the Sergeant Major, and Fitz and the Gogg the Escorts.

The trial took place at 2000hrs(8pm). Poppa sat at the Signal Officer's table, Feathers stood behind and a little to the right of Poppa. I was elected to be the prisoner's friend and Horrie and I had to wait outside the door with an escort on each side.

'Ready Sergeant Major,' from the Adjutant. The Sergeant Major opened the door, 'Prisoner and Escort, attention, right turn, quick march,' this movement brought us in line to the CO's table.

Sergeant Major:'Right turn, halt, escort stand at ease.' The prisoner's friend to Sergeant Major, 'May the prisoner be seated' Sergeant Major to the Adjutant 'May the prisoner sit down, Sir'. Adjutant to the CO 'Permission is asked for the prisoner to be seated.' The CO: 'Certainly not, the prisoner will stand to attention.' The prisoner's friend: 'That is impossible Sir, if the prisoner places both sets of feet at the position of attention he is unable to balance, if you see what I mean Sir.' The CO: 'Nothing swift will be put over here, demonstrate that I might see...'

As requested I closed Horrie's feet in together and toppled him over, Horrie thought this good fun and he wriggled on his back. "Enough," said the CO, 'The prisoner in these highly unusual circumstances may be seated.' I sat Horrie at my feet. The CO to the Adjutant; 'Now I can't see the prisoner.' The Adjutant:'Elevate the prisoner so he may be seen by the old fox.' The CO turned sharply to the Adjutant, 'What was that?' The Adjutant: 'I suggested to place the prisoner on a box.' 'Very good.' The Sergeant Major produced a packing case and I sat Horrie on it facing the CO. The Adjutant picked up the charge sheet from the table and read to Horrie: 'EXI, Cpl Horrie the Wog Dog HQ

Coy 2/1ˢᵗ M/G Btn, are these your particulars?' 'Yes,' I replied. The CO: 'The prisoner will answer himself to his own particulars.'

Horrie looked from one face to the other, the serious tone of voice had him tricked a bit.

The prisoners friend: 'Sir the prisoner is an 'Egyptian Italian' and no speaka da English too good.'

The CO:'Rubbish. Are you Horrie the Wog Dog?' Horrie agreed with a grin and tail wag. 'Wipe that grin from your face Cpl,' said the CO sternly. Horrie stopped grinning and cocked his head on one side and looked inquiringly at the CO. The CO to the Adjutant: 'Read the charge to the prisoner.' The Adjutant to Horrie: 'You are charged under Army Act 15, that you did, whilst on active service, absent yourself from your place of camp without leave, from 0530 hrs on 20ᵗʰ Dec. 1941 until 1600 hrs on 21ˢᵗ Dec 1941.'

The Adjutant handed the paper to the CO. The CO lifted his gaze to Horrie and asked, 'Cpl, how do you plead to this charge?' 'How do you plead?' I asked, bending down to speak to him. Horrie endeavoured to lick my face. To the CO: 'Sir the prisoner pleads guilty but with an explanation.' The CO looks through some papers, 'Cpl you have been with this unit a long time now...' (tail wags from the prisoner) 'You have been a good soldier Horrie,' (very many wags) 'But you must set an example to Imshee.'

Horrie jumped down from the box and made for the door.

The Sergeant Major: 'Horrie, stand fast!' Horrie stopped and looked back. Sergeant Major: 'Escort the prisoner to his seat.' Horrie was returned to his former position. The CO: 'This is highly irregular.' The prisoners friend: 'Sir, I beg leniency for the prisoner as his girlfriend's name distracts him.' The CO: ' Very well, what is your explanation for this leave of absence?' 'Sir, I speak for the prisoner.' The CO: 'Continue' 'Sir, I was lead astray by that careless Moody.' Cries of 'Informer' from the Escort. 'Silence,' roared the CO. The CO to Horrie: 'Cpl that's no excuse, it's not good enough, I have no option but to reduce you to the ranks with the loss of bones for one day.' 'Horrie,' I told him, 'You lose your stripes and forfeit your bones for one day.' I removed Horrie's stripes but he didn't seem to mind. 'Do you wish to tell Imshee,' I asked him. Apparently he did, as he made for the door I opened it. 'Off you go Private Horrie,' laughed Poppa. Horrie disappeared into the darkness.

When the snow started to fall Horrie and Imshee had a great time scampering about, Horrie would return to our tent with his uniform sopping wet, invariably he would ask someone to remove it for him.

He accomplished this by attracting the attention of one of the Sigs. by standing on his hind legs and placing his two front paws on their leg then jumping up and down and shaking himself. While removing the coat he would lick the hand in appreciation. It was seldom that he would venture out without his coat, at night it was hung up to dry on a rack near the heater. Horrie got to know the early morning routine and he would not accompany us outside into the cold when we went for an early morning wash.

Later when we went out for duty or parades he knew we would not be returning for awhile, as we prepared to go out he would take up position alongside his coat and when anyone took it down to put it on for him, his little growl of pleasure and much tail wagging showed that he wished his coat to be put on. Should by any strange chance we be running late and forget his coat he would not budge from his position alongside his coat but loudly bark his disapproval at this forgetfulness.

When the snow set in and the soft snow became a hard icy surface, Horrie's pads soon played up. We made canvas boots for him but they annoyed him so much we had to discard them. Keeping his pads heavily smeared with Vaseline was of no use either. He used to look so mournful being left in the hut that I suggested to the Rebels that if we had a sledge Horrie would be able to travel with us. Also we could place the signal gear on it that we often had to carry for miles when checking over the telephone lines in the valley.

As we were often out all day, a Billy, etc could be carted also. It proved an excellent idea. The sledge was a light rough affair made from a sheet of 6 by 3 wood, the sides were turned up to a depth of about 12ins. At the turned-up front we built a box for Horrie so that he would not bounce about with the signal gear and ration tins, etc. An old blanket was put in the bottom of the box and after we had warmed up he also had our greatcoats to help keep him warm. He dearly loved this cosy method of travelling and when on the move he would sit up, his little head would just show above the upturned front. We were never able to persuade Imshee to sit in with him as she probably did not have the trust in us that Horrie did. She would accompany us by trotting alongside Horrie in the sledge until just out of the camp area, then she would return. Horrie would turn round and watch her until she disappeared into the distance.

We never needed much excuse to get the old Billy boiling for a cup of tea but as Horrie showed no special liking for warm tea we dubbed in and got a large tin of Horlicks for him, he had an old mug that always travelled with the sledge and while we enjoyed a brew of tea, Horrie was never forgotten and he joined us with his warm mug of Horlicks. At times we had to leave the sledge on one side of a little creek that wound along the centre of the valley while we checked the line on the opposite side of the creek; Horrie was always left in charge of the sledge and it was impossible for any native to get anywhere near our gear.

Horrie used to perform a very valuable service by carrying the wireless news from our Signal Office to Mac's hut, it only required one hour to teach him to perform this task. Mac provided an old leather pouch and starting from the Sig. Office I made Horrie understand to carry it in his mouth, after dropping it a few times he quickly caught the idea of holding it in his mouth. He accompanied me to Macs hut where Mac was waiting for him, leading Horrie up to Mac, Mac gently took the pouch and patted him, telling him he was a good dog, leaving Horrie with Mac I would return to the Sig. Office and Mac would repeat the performance from his end, receiving it also I patted him and praised him, by this time he was quite keen. The second lesson commenced by Mac and I standing about 110 yards apart, giving Horrie the pouch I would say 'give it to Mac' and waving to Mac he would call Horrie, this procedure was repeated again from Mac's end. We gradually increased distance between us until Horrie would carry it from the Sig. office to Mac's hut and back again.

The final tryout without Mac or I calling him and also both of us out of sight was performed correctly the first time. The first message from the Sig. hut was written down on a piece of paper and put into the pouch, the wording was 'Here she comes, I hope.' Giving the pouch to Horrie who was now as keen as mustard and jumping up and down in his excitement, I said "Give it to Mac," and off he trotted. He arrived back with the reply 'Received okay, pop over for a brew of tea on receipt.' Horrie and I popped over for tea and Horlicks. From then on the pouch was always kept in the Sig. Office and never used for any other purpose than a message for Mac. I had only to show Horrie the pouch and he would prance about and bark his willingness to carry a message.

At this time news was eagerly awaited. The loss of the *Prince of Wales* and the *Repulse* had keyed the troops up, also it was reported that some elements of the 6th Division were now in action against the Japs. Gordie rigged our issue wireless up so that we could pick up Reuters news in Morse code from London, we jotted it down then re-wrote several sheets to be passed outside the Sig. Office for the news. A separate sheet was put into the pouch and given to Horrie.

The crowd outside the Sig. hut would always give the little dog gangway as he trotted proudly across to the Anti-Tank lines with the news, on arrival there he always received a small reward and while eating this small reward Mac would scribble a note for Horrie to bring back'Received okay thanks.' In this manner Mac's friends received all the important news via the wog dog, he did not fail to deliver the message on any occasion and the crowning triumph came one night when he arrived back accompanied by Imshee, he was determined to exercise his duty before taking his pleasure.

Another little job he used to perform for me was to bring my boots from the heater in the centre of the hut to my bed in the mornings. The floor of the hut consisted of square concrete slabs and consequently pretty cold to the bare feet. My bed was at the end of the hut, it consisted of three wide planks resting on a box at each end, the box at the foot of the bed was Horrie's kennel. Boots were placed on a rack near the heater to dry overnight. I always tied mine together with the laces and placed them not on the rack but on the floor at the back of the rack.

Teaching Horrie to do this little service was very easy, I made him accompany me each time I walked from my bed to the heater to place the boots, I would say to him 'my boots' then giving him the laces between the boots I would say 'fetch them' He was unable to lift the boots but he could drag them along. He was quick to learn and after getting his front feet tangled up with the boots a few times he got the idea to turn around and back them towards my bed.

On reveille I would crawl to the end of my bed and look into his box 'Hey my boots please?' and he immediately got the boots for me saving a walk on the cold floor. Of course the Rebels made many rude suggestions about the boots. One remark suggested that there was no need for me to put my boots on in a separate place from the rest as Horrie could easily tell which were mine.

The usual signs of a move being on started to appear about the 20th January, the telephone became very busy, special Don R's carrying urgent dispatches arrived at the Sig. Office more often than was usual. Boxes to stow gear in were being made and repaired by our unit carpenters and numerous other signs now very familiar to us pointed to a move. The news from Malaya was not bright and the boys were getting anxious about the position in the Pacific. Of our ultimate destination the Rebels were all sure it was to be Australia or Malaya except Big Jim and Poppa. Discussions took place in our Sig. hut almost every night. While we were waiting for Reuters news from London, quite often Poppa and Big Jim joined in the discussions.

From the very beginning the rebel section had adopted the motto of the Doc H Club, that being 'Abandon rank all ye who enter here' this applied to the Sig. Officer also when the rebel section were on duty there. Big Jim and Poppa always entered into the spirit of the Doc H during these informal chats.

A lengthy discussion took place one night among the Rebels, Big Jim and Poppa.

As I believe it was a fair representation of feelings of the troops I will jot down what I recall of it as it may possibly be of interest.

The news had been handed out and the Rebels were talking things over when Big Jim came into the Sig. Office. "The news is not so hot," I remarked to him. "No she certainly isn't," he replied.

"We were saying that we hope they move us to Malaya or Australia," said Fitz. "Do you think you should go home?" remarked Big Jim. Feathers replied he was sorry now that he ever left Aussie. Poppa replied to this remark, "Whoever thought the Japs would come into the war when we left for overseas?"

Gordie replied that the 'Chocos' did apparently. "Perhaps, but I doubt it" replied Poppa," for instance see if you can give me one reason each why you joined the A.I.F knowing that you would probably leave Aussie, lets start with our good friend Big Jim.

"Okay" replied Big Jim, "Firstly Britain was at war, Australia is part of the British Empire as you know and apart from us being Aussies we are of British stock, we are British and although you make fun of the Tommies and the Old Dart you are bloody proud of being British, agree?"

'Yes' we grinned.

"Well then I suggest we were all willing to be used as England wished us to be used, in fact your swore on Attestation to fight the King's enemies at all times, correct?" "Yes," we replied.

"But now that Australia is closer to the war you wish to drop everything here and return home, is that right?" he asked. "Certainly is," we replied. "Well then why did you not join the Militia instead of the A.I.F - you!" first pointing to me. "Okay," I replied, "It had been pumped into us that the position in the Pacific was secure, some of the reasons being that firstly America had considerable interests in the Pacific and could therefore not afford to let the Japs get control of the Pacific, and whoever compared the Japs to the Yanks, secondly, Japan relied upon the USA for about eighty percent of her petrol and oil, thirdly, she depended upon Britain for rubber"; and, chipped in Don, "Australia for scrap iron in spite of the Wharfies."

"Well," I continued, "She certainly relied on Aussie for wool anyway, fourthly, Japan had been at war with China for about five years, her planes were no good, her pilots not so hot, owing to their diets they were poor flyers; for these reasons I had no fear of leaving Aussie but as I was like many others, poorly informed about the strength of Japan I consider it our duty to return to Malaya or anywhere we can get at the Japs, who are actually Australia's number one enemy, apart from being an enemy of Britain; carry on Fitz," I asked.

"I agree entirely with Jim and add that we have at home only the Militia who are not yet proved, while away from home we have the men who have actually had some experience in warfare, the Militia may be good, personally I don't think so, but the fact remains we have not got sufficient troops to defend Australia even if the A.I.F returns, we are well trained and fit and don't forget we are also Australians, I say we should return home."

Gordie, 'she's all yours.' "I fall into line with Fitz and Jim and add that we can expect little help from England, she is dead up against the wall already as you will agree, I am sure we will have to depend almost entirely on the USA for help but at least we can supply 4 Divvies of A.I.F troops to help defend our own soil." 'Your go Feathers.' "Malaya, Java or Australia I say," he replied, "we have willingly and quickly given England all the help we possibly could, now we are needed nearer to home and we should out of all fairness to us be sent there."

Don, 'your turn.' "I agree with the rest of the mob, we have done what we possibly could wherever England has used us, we certainly have not been spared nor did we ask or wish to be spared, we were given an impossible task in Greece but the Tommies shared in that task also, I have no complaints to make if they send us home, if we are not returned I reckon we are the suckers, England may not be able to help much in the Pacific but at least she could get us back in that area."

'Okay Gogg.' "My people and my home is in Australia and if there is likely to be anything doing there I want to be there also, anyway we are doing nothing here except to be handy in case, we have only three Divisions in the Middle East; surely we could be replaced easily enough. What about the thousands of troops in England, they are there because of the danger of invasion I suppose; well there is danger of invasion in Australia also, three Divvies are not much here but three Divvies would make a hell of a difference back home."

"Well, the Rebels seem to have unity anyway" Big Jim opened up, "But I see it this way, first of all don't get me wrong as nobody would like a crack at the Japs more than I would, but you forget first of all we have Singapore and this is a pain in the neck for the Japs as far as the West Coast is concerned. Then again we now have an active American Pacific Fleet, the small but pugnacious Aussie Navy plus the ships of the R.N and don't forget we have the 8th Divvy in Malaya plus goodness knows how many troops; so my way of thinking you blokes panic too soon. We are eminently suited for warfare in the desert as most of our training has been done there and don't forget a big job is still to be done in Africa and this means as much to Australia as it does to England, our homes are in Aussie you say, well the Tommies over here have homes in England and the Germans are a damn sight closer to the Tommies homes than the Japs are to ours.

"I think that the Jerry is still our number one enemy. America, apart from being a Democracy like ourselves would never let the Japs get a hold on Australia. She also has huge financial interests there, then again you admit that England is up against it, could she spare the shipping plus naval escort to remove three Divvies from the Middle East to the Far East in a hurry? Three Divvies take a fair bit of handling, don't forget and apart from this the Yanks plus equipment will be pouring into Aussie, so I say our job is not necessarily a local one and my guess is that we will return to the Western Desert."

'What say you Poppa?' "I agree that the move is more likely to be the Western Desert," he replied.

Big Jim laughed: "Poppa and I to the desert and the Rebels to the Far East, what about Horrie?" "The wog dog goes with us," we replied, "and after we clean the Japs up we will come back and give you a hand." "Okay," he laughed, "When do you start?" "As soon as I get my gear packed," replied Feathers.

The day of the move arrived and as we were requested to hand in all our warm gear such as balaclavas, etc. We guessed the move to be the warmer south to start with anyway. It was a Tommy unit that took over our position and they were all sure that we would return home. We got underway before the Anti-Tank Regiment and Horrie watched Imshee in Mac's arms until we were out of sight. He was very miserable for a few days and in spite of the excitement of moving again he fretted for Imshee. As we continued south we passed many Tommy units moving north to take over our former positions. "Sorry to lose you Aussie," they called. "We'll be back!" we replied and every man meant it. It was the same fight, Britain's fight, but for us in a different theatre until we were able to return again.

Arriving back in Palestine we were to wait some eight weeks before the next move. The days passed very slowly, the 8th Divvy were now in the thick of it and the news continued to be dull and not at all to our liking. The troops were unsettled, leave did not appeal to many and the leisure hours were spent in camp discussing the various aspects of the war in the Far East.

Some invented a game to help brighten and pass the long hours of waiting. They called the game 'Racing Beetles.' A large circle about 4 foot in diameter was clearly marked on the ground. Placed in the centre of the circle was a round cake tin that had both the top and bottom removed. Each player selected and caught his own beetle and after it being approved by the judge as eligible to start, it was marked with a piece of chalk, red or blue ink and grey paint etc. Each beetle had to be some breed and approximately the same size, the usual beetle used was an ugly black little blighter called the Scarab, once the holy beetle of ancient Egypt and was worshipped as such.

Each beetle cost 200 mils to start in the race, the owner of the winning beetle scooping the pool. Each entry after being approved by the judge was put into the empty cake tin together with 200 mils. The race was run by the judge lifting the tin up and allowing the beetles to scurry in all directions. The first beetle across the line marking the circle was the winner and its lucky owner collected the 'doings' (pool) After each race the winner was removed and not permitted to race again. Quite a lot of fun and amusement was obtained from this sport of Kings and the calls of 'Come on Phar Lap,' etc added to the fun.

Fitz introduced to our tent Cuthbert Mark 1, Cuthbert Mark 1 was a small chameleon some six inches long, these strange little lizards looked like miniature prehistoric reptiles. Their eyes worked independently to each other, often one looking ahead and the other astern. They had feet that looked more suitable for climbing trees than walking on the desert as they appeared like a claw. This movement was also queer as they walked in a hesitating manner placing one foot forward then moving the body backwards and forwards three or four times before advancing the other leg. Fitz reckoned they were unable to make up their minds.

They had tongues as long as their bodies and they could flick it out and roll it back like a kid's squeaker. At the end of the tongue there appeared a hard sticky substance and they could pick a fly off and return it to their large mouth from a distance of 6 inches without fail.

The Rebels soon produced Cuthbert Mark 2 and 3. The three competitors stalked around the tent with their chameleons perched upon the index finger and on sighting a fly, the finger was pointed at the unsuspecting victim, of course angle shots and upside down shots were indulged in to impress the spectators with the powers of Cuthbert Mark 1, 2 and 3. Cuthbert Mark 2 was the best as he could consume 20 flies before refusing an offered victim. Mark 1 was the next best with 12 flies while Mark 3 was a poor doer and could only manage 8 flies at one sitting. When not in use they were kept in a box at the foot of the tent pole. Horrie was very jealous of these other pets and he would look longingly at them in the box but as he was told not to touch them he exerted his will power. Fitz made his chameleon earn its tucker by putting such vivid colours as blue and red into the box, Feathers reckoned he would eventually have the poor chameleons turning inside out trying to keep up with Fitz changing colour so often.

Arising one morning I noticed Horrie had a rather hang-dog look about him and as I went near the chameleon's box Horrie rolled over on his back. Looking into the box confirmed my suspicion, the temptation had at last overcome the wog dog's will power. Fitz must have noticed me looking in the box as he sat up in bed

"Finish Cuthbert Mark 1?" he enquired.

"Finish Cuthbert 1, 2 and 3," I replied.

"Horrie, you little cannibal!" he scolded.

Horrie still lying on his back wagged his tail.

Horrie in those days in Palestine had lost some of his enthusiasm and he spent many hours lying quietly on the foot of my bed. All the Rebels and Poppa noticed it and although all knew that Horrie's fate must soon become a real thing we avoided speaking about it. Quite a few of the boys would drop in for a chat and invariably pat Horrie and exclaim, 'Poor little Horrie,' 'Poor little wog dog.' It seems strange but Horrie would watch us talking, his little head resting on his front paw and his eyes looked sad and searching. Feathers broke the ice by saying, "Do you know I'm getting that way that I hardly like to look Horrie in the face."

As Feathers made this remark Poppa came into the tent. "This joint is like a flaming morgue," he exclaimed and picking Horrie up he continue, "Even the little wog dog has got the miseries." "I think Horrie knows his days in the A.I.F will soon be over," I said, stroking Horrie's head gently. The Rebels were all quiet. "Yes," replied Poppa "It's a damn shame to leave the little bloke behind, I remember just before we returned home after the last war the Australian soldiers shot their beloved horses rather than leave them in the hands of the natives, and I can tell you there was many a lump in the throat of the old diggers." "Guess it was better to destroy them than have them worked to death by the wogs," declared Fitz. During this conversation Poppa was holding Horrie in his arms and as he was sitting next to me on the edge of my bed Horrie was able to nose my arm. "What's up little dog?" I asked him. If Horrie had been able to speak I know he would have begged not to be left behind.

"What would the position be if we got caught trying to get Horrie home with us?" I asked. "If we actually got him home I think we could manage to leave him in Quarantine," replied Poppa, "But if he was discovered before we got home he would be pretty sure to be destroyed." "Well if we leave him behind it would be best to destroy him anyway," replied Fitz, "So at least by giving it a fly he has a fighting chance." "Surely the little chap is entitled to a chance no matter how slender it is," remarked Gordie. "He has been quite prepared to take his chance with us before this," I replied. Horrie listened to all this very quietly. "Cheer up little dog we won't let you down," remarked the Gogg, walking over to Poppa and patting Horrie. "It will be no easy task getting him home," remarked Gordie, "One little step and Horrie's faithfulness goes unrewarded." "There will be no slip," I remarked, "But we will need our entire efforts to work for this result and I think it the least we should do for the little dog."

All the Rebels and Poppa agreed. I suggested that we get a Vet to look Horrie over then we need have no fear of him being unfit to enter Australia. They agreed it would be the right thing to do. "You seem quite sure we are going home," remarked Poppa. The Rebels at this stage of the game had no doubt. Poppa agreed to fix it for Don and myself to get leave to Tel Aviv the following day as our first step was to make sure Horrie was in perfect health.

The following morning Don Horrie and I set out for Tel Aviv, we eventually located a very small shop that sold all manner of things that a dog owner might require. I inquired if there was a Vet at the shop but however they gave us the address of a Vet in Allenby Road. We found the home of the Vet without much trouble and the Vet himself opened the door in answer to our knock. We were greeted by a kindly grey-haired elderly man who spoke fluent English. During our conversation with him we were to learn that he was a refugee Jew from Berlin. He and his family had been forced to leave Germany and they eventually arrived here in Palestine. At the age of 65 he had to start his life's work all over again. A Doctor and a Veterinary Surgeon in Germany, he had followed his profession in Tel Aviv and had started to build up a practice again.

"What can I do for you" he asked after opening the door "Well it's rather a long story" I replied. He invited us in to his small waiting room, a writing desk, few chairs and a table heaped with books greeted us, along one wall there were two shelves filled with Medical books but I particularly noticed that the three pictures that graced the room were of animals, one of a huge Russian wolfhound and the other two of horses.

Don and I were invited to be seated and I held Horrie in my arms. "Now my friends tell me of your troubles," he smiled. "Well," I began, "We have had this little dog for over twelve months now and he has accompanied us wherever we have been. He was in Greece and Crete also with us, and part of his adventures were on a ship that was bombed and sunk. To make a long story short we are very attached to the little chap and as some day we might return to Australia we would like to take him also.

"Officially we would be unable to take him owing to the rigid quarantine regulations but unofficially we intend to try. Our main worry is this, if by any chance the dog has any disease we will have no option but to destroy him rather than leave him behind, but if he is given a clean bill of health we will certainly try to get him home and be hanged to the consequences."

Horrie sat quietly in my lap and watched the face of the vet. The Vet smiled, "Let me have a look at him." He came round from behind the desk towards me, I placed Horrie on the floor. The Vet first offered Horrie the back of his hand to smell, Horrie sniffed cautiously. Very quietly and slowly the Vet placed his other hand on Horrie's head and gently patted him. Horrie trusted him entirely and before long the Vet picked him up and placed him on the table. He examined the inside of Horrie's ears smelling them at the same time. "Quite clean," he observed. "Is the dog subject to fits?" he enquired. No was the answer. He put Horrie down on the floor and turned to me, "Your little dog seems to be healthy but I would like you to leave him with me for a few days as I would like to make several tests and observe him," he told me.

I looked at Don and hesitated. "He will be quite alright I assure you," the Vet continued, "Let me show you a few of my patients." Conducting us through the house we were taken to the backyard. It was divided up into small runs completely covered with a wire frame, each run had a kennel at one end and about five of the runs had inmates. "Your little dog will remain here," he said, indicating a vacant run. I placed Horrie in the run he indicated and Don and I spoke to him 'Good dog Horrie!' "Can you leave some personal article until you return for the dog?" he enquired. Thinking that he wanted a deposit and not holding too good I started to remove my watch. "No," the Vet said,"Not your watch, a sock would serve the purpose admirably," he continued. "What on earth for?" I asked getting a little suspicious. "If you leave a sock with your little dog he will not fret so much at your absence," he explained, "He will treasure the article with your scent upon it and expect you to return." I removed my boot and put the sock inside the cage for Horrie. "We shall leave him now," said the Vet, leading us back to the house 'Good dog' Don and I said repeatedly as we walked towards the back door.

Poor Horrie stood looking at us through the wire, he was very miserable. Advising that we would return the following Monday we left the Vet and the little wog dog. Don and I made our way to the Australian Soldiers Club to wait there until the leave bus arrived to take us back to camp. "Poor little wog dog, I didn't like leaving him," I remarked. "No, I didn't either," replied Don, "But I think he will be well looked after. Good idea about the sock." I replied that I hoped Horrie got more comfort from it than I was getting without it, which reminds me, I added, "Don't tell the Rebels anything about the sock as I will never hear the end of it." "Okay," laughed Don.

After returning to the Rebels we related all that had happened except about the sock, they all agreed that it was a good idea. Feathers remarked that if Horrie has anything wrong with him I'll bet we have it also. We missed the little wog dog very much during the next seven days and often we would ask each other 'Wonder how Horrie is?' Several of the troops noticed Horrie was missing and enquired where the little wog dog was. We told them he was AWL again but would probably turn up again before long.

At last the day arrived and Poppa wangled it so I could have a truck for a few hours to get into Tel Aviv.

My knock was answered again by the Vet and I could tell immediately by his smile that all was well.

Ushering me again into the waiting room he remarked, "Well I suppose you are anxious about your little Dog?" "Yes," I replied. "Well let us get him first," he added. I called Horrie as the Vet opened the back door, Horrie shot out of his kennel very excited and jumped up and down against the wire netting that separated us. The Vet unlocked the door and Horrie scampered round and round nearly wagging himself in half. The Vet informed me that Horrie remained with the sock all the time. If he went into the kennel he would take the sock with him. Returning to the waiting room with the wagging pup under my arms the Vet told me he was totally unable to trace signs of any canine disease. "You need have no fear," he advised me, "Your little dog is in excellent health, If anything prevents you from taking him with you I will readily accept him... You have a very faithful little friend here," patting Horrie. Horrie was all wags. The Vet would accept nothing as a fee for his services and wished me the best of luck. As we reached the front door I asked him if he had any idea what breed Horrie was.

He smiled and replied "Just a nice little dog!" "Well we don't care, do we Horrie?" I asked the wog dog. Horrie didn't have a care in the world. Thanking the kindly Vet I sincerely wished him good luck and the little no-breed dog and I walked out to the truck.

During the run back to the camp Horrie stood on my lap and placed his two front paws on the top of the door, putting his head out the window he joyously barked at everything we passed. Parking the truck in the transport lines I hurried over to the Rebels tent with Horrie well in the lead, his excited bark brought Don to the door of the tent who picked up the excited wriggling dog. The Rebels gathered round him and all tried to pat and talk to the little dog together, Horrie's stub tail wagged in top gear. "He's okay," I told them. 'You beaut!' was the chorus from the Rebels. I repeated what the Vet had told me. "Number one hurdle over safely," remarked Gordie who now had hold of the pup. "Personally I thought it was a certainty," remarked Feathers, "But anyway now we know for certain."

Poppa came over to hear the news "Good show" he replied, "But I have some news also; Khassa the L.A.D dog was whizzed off this morning so I would keep an eye on Horrie from now on." There and then we decided not to let Horrie wander about by himself and if he went out at all at least one of the Rebels must accompany him.

Near our last camp in Palestine at Hill 95 there was a large iron structure built for the troops as a Picture Theatre. There being many troops in this area it was necessary to have two sessions to enable all to be accommodated. The first at 5.30pm and the second at 8pm. It was the habit of the Rebels to attend the first session and as Horrie was never allowed out of our sigh, he was taken along to the pictures. Forming up in a long queue for seats he would gradually move forward with us and was the object of much amusement to the troops who noticed the little dog patiently waiting his turn to pass the ticket window and into the door. One of us would always pick him up as we entered and we always sat together. During the picture he was amusing to watch, by standing on our knees and placing his front feet on top of the backrest of the seat in front, he was just tall enough to see the screen. Often the ear of the cove in front got a lick just for luck and if he had not previously noticed the dog before, this friendly gesture on Horrie's part would often bring him up with a yell. His interest in the pictures was amazing, if by any chance a dog or animal appeared on the screen he would bark his excitement much to the amusement of the boys, when very excited he would scramble along the platform of knees. At half time he always received his 'snow' the name of an ice-cream, he thoroughly enjoyed this refreshment. One of the Rebels would hold the cone while Horrie licked the ice-cream in the approved manner, the little stub tail keeping time to the pink tongue.

He got to know the time when we were due to move from the camp to the Picture Theatre. One night for some reason or other we had decided to go to the second sitting instead of the first. As the usual time for us to go approached Horrie got very excited. When we made no move he visited one after the other telling us it was time for the pictures, but as he was unable to persuade us to move he became very offended and sat down giving us each a scornful look in turn. When the time arrived for the second sitting the Gogg mentioned the word 'pictures' - Horrie was up on his feet in a flash and wagging his little tail in pleasure. "Strike me, the little bloke even knows the word 'pictures'!", remarked Poppa.

The news from Malaya was getting steadily worse, the 8th Divvy were being pushed back to our amazement and soon we were to read the words: 'The position in Singapore is grave', 'Singapore Fell, Singapore Gone.' We could scarcely believe it. No longer was it a matter of going home but could we get back to Australia in time to be of use, could they get us there before the Japs landed. The troops were seething with impatience to get home. 'Never mind the convoy, anything at all will do but for God's sake hurry.' 'What the hell are they doing?' 'Why this bloody delay?' 'Singapore lost and the 8th Divvy in the Japs hands!' 'Something radically wrong somewhere!' Rumours flew thick and fast. 'The Aussie coastal ships were coming to take us home.' 'Lord Haw Haw said the Australians were about to finish in a watery grave.' 'Well maybe he is right but for goodness sake make some effort to get us home.'

The days passed but still no sign of a move, troops continued to come down from Syria and Happy MacMillan and his Regiment arrived and camped alongside our unit. Taking Horrie over to see them, I explained Happy was the reason for Horrie losing his stripes. Horrie accepted their apologies with many wags of his tail assuring them that he didn't mind as it made no difference to his rations anyway.

We arranged a football match between the A-A Reg. and the Mug-gunners. As I was playing, the Rebels held Horrie who barked his encouragement to our side. However, the ball bounced near where the Rebels were sitting and a sudden unexpected jerk on the lead and Horrie joined the game. He caught the ball and bounced it off his chest, with a yelp of excitement he followed it up again, the players all stopped and roared laughing. Shouts of encouragement from the mob got Horrie right into top form! He didn't play for any particular side and tripping on his trailing lead only encouraged him all the more. Moving across to him I picked him up and held him above my head, cheers from all the spectators and players rewarded his effort, and still full of enthusiasm I handed the wog dog back to Don who came out to retrieve him.

The A-A Reg. got word that night they were moving out early next morning so presuming we might be next, we immediately called a council among the Rebels to discuss plans for Horrie's future.

Poppa and all the Rebels took part in discussing the ways and means to evolve a water tight plan to get the wog dog home. "It would be better if Horrie disappeared some little time before the actual move," I suggested, "As this would probably help to avoid suspicion." "Yes that's a good suggestion," replied Poppa, "Everyone knows of the Rebels attachment for their little dog as well as their reputation, consequently one and all will suspect that you will try to smuggle him home," he continued. "If we can find some way of keeping Horrie away from camp, but yet be near enough for us to pick him up in a hurry should the move arrive unexpectedly." "I think it would be a good move," suggested Don. "Yes, but that's a bit difficult," replied Feathers, "There is no one near here that we could leave Horrie with except wogs and Horrie wouldn't stand for that." "What method of transport do you suggest for smuggling him onto the ship?" inquired the Gogg. "Wait a moment," replied Poppa, "Let's get one problem settled at a time, you all agree that it is best for Horrie to disappear before orders come out to the effect that all pets have to be destroyed?" 'Yes,' we all agreed to this for a start. "Okay then, lets have some suggestions as to how we are going to arrange this," replied Poppa.

Feathers suggested that perhaps we could hide Horrie during the day in a slit trench in the vacated Ack-Ack area. This seemed a fairly good suggestion as the Ack-Ack mob were moving out and their area was fairly close to us. In fact it was alongside our area, but a small hill between the two camps kept each out of sight from the other. Fitz pointed out the possibility that anyone wandering across the area might spot Horrie in the trench. Yes, we agreed, that might be fatal. Don suggested that we could take it turns to keep the trench under observation from the hill that separated the camps, and if they spotted anyone walking towards the trench the observers could head them off without attracting attention to the fact. Poppa added that he could arrange the duties so that at least one rebel could be free to act as the observer.

We agreed to this plan pending any better idea that we might hit upon. "Okay for that much, now what about the explanation as to Horrie's absence," enquired Poppa. "This needs to be pretty good," remarked the Gogg, "As there will be plenty of inquiries." "Could we say he got skittled by a truck when we were returning from the pictures?" suggested Gordie." "It sounds a bit obvious though, especially as this is the all important move," replied Don. I suggested that we dig a hole outside our tent and fill it again immediately, then we could say Horrie was buried there, also we could get the Gogg to paint Horrie's name on a little cross.

This appealed for a few moments. Don remarked that we could all appear upset over Horrie being killed and so set the plan off. Gordie found the fault. It was possible but not probable that anyone being suspicious could order the grave to be uncovered, then the game was up and no matter what we devised after that it would almost be hopeless.

It was most unlikely that this order would be given but there must be absolutely no chances taken. "Why not say we have given him to some English people in Tel Aviv?" suggested Fitz. "No good," replied Feathers, "They could check this up also." "Well then," suggested Fitz again, "What about saying that we gave him to a Palestinian policeman in Tel

Aviv but we do not know his address. Then Horrie could be in anyone of the numerous Police block houses in Palestine, they could hardly be likely to check them all." "Yes that's alright, but they may not believe us and be more suspicious than ever," replied Poppa.

"I've got it!" I exclaimed, "We will actually give Horrie to the Palestinian police, in fact I will get one of the Regimental Provost to accompany Horrie and I to the block house at the beach near Ascalon. I can arrange to whiz him back alright," I added. "But how?" asked Poppa. "Well," I replied, "I'm pretty sure they will accept him, then after awhile I will return and tell them we want him for a unit photograph and simply forget to take him back." "Yes," replied Gordie "But what if we should have to move in a hurry at night, what excuse could you think of if you had to call at say 2am and ask for the dog and what's more you may not be able to get over to Ascalon and back in time!"

I asked Poppa how much notice we were likely to get and he replied probably 24 hours notice to move. "Okay," I replied, "Can you fix it for me to get away for an hour or so in the morning?" "Sure," he replied, "Well I think I can manage, I will be able to let you know as soon as I get back. If it works out like I think it will, we will actually give Horrie to the Police tomorrow and just to make sure I will get him back again the same night." "That should be fairly safe if you can manage it." Poppa replied. "Well," I answered, "I will know for certain after I see them in the morning." I had a rough plan in mind but wished to think out a few details. "So far so good..." remarked Poppa, "We can keep Horrie hidden and we have an extra good explanation for his absence." The Gogg upset the scheme by asking "Suppose we have a full unit muster parade, which is likely, there being an invasion, and while the trench is not under observation some stranger sees Horrie and let him out." "Finish slit trench," remarked Fitz. "Pity we couldn't keep him in the tent somehow." "What about keeping him in one of the Signal boxes in the tent?" enquired the Gogg. "No," replied Poppa, "Tent inspection might be fatal."

The inspiration came from Don. "Look" he cried, pointing to the cane mat that served me as a bed; "A hole under Jim's bed." 'You beaut!' was the chorus. Investigating the mat we found we could afford to dig a hole about 5 foot long and 2 foot wide and have a fair bit of matting left over to cover the edge of the hole. "To work, my hearty signalers!" called Poppa, "We can prepare the hiding place now and if Jim's plan about the coppers works out okay we will be all set for Horrie's return tomorrow night."

We rolled the mat up and made a start. Poppa was appointed nit-keeper of the door just in case anyone should approach our tent. We possessed only one spade in the tent but the sand was easy digging. After we outlined the hole the problem arose, what can we do with the sand removed from the hole?

The sand below would be moist and a shade different colour to the fine dry sand on the surface, to throw it outside was just inviting an inquiry as to where it came from. However Poppa produced a bucket from outside the tent and this was used to remove the surplus sand from the hole.

Fortunately our tent was on the outskirts and although we had other tents in front and on each side, there were none in the rear. Poppa retained his post at the door while Fitz and Gordie kept watch on the tent either side. Don and Feather's took it in turn to dig the hole.

I took up position at the rear of the tent and kept close to the flap. After getting the all clear from the nit-keepers, the Gogg passed the bucket under the flap to me and I cautiously crept to an old slit trench on the side of the small hill at the rear of our tent; the trench approximately 15 yards from the rear of the tent. I silently emptied the bucket into the trench then returning handed the bucket under the flap to the waiting Gogg. It took a considerable number of buckets full before the hole was large enough. After emptying the last bucket I scraped the fine dry sand over the wet sand in the slit trench hoping that in the morning the trench would appear as though it had been half-filled in for some time.

The area where I had scraped the dry sand from I smoothed over with a stick to make it appear undisturbed. Returning to the tent I found that my bed presented a hole 5 foot long by 2 foot wide and about 5 foot deep. So far so good. Feathers, Don and I went out and scrounged several lengths of packing crate boards. These boards were crisscrossed over the hole and sunk in each side of the hole. The ends of the boards, where they protruded out past the covering mat, were covered over with sand.

When the mat was rolled out the job was perfect and not one in one thousand would have suspected that the mat concealed a hole. We decided that we would wait until the following night before training Horrie to stay quietly in the hole. We now had prepared the perfect hiding place, if Horrie would play his part as carefully as we did.

The precautions we took may seem extraordinary but Horrie was an extraordinary little dog and what's more he is home in Australia.

We were all very pleased with the progress so far and the next step depended upon the arrangements I could make the following morning with the Palestinian police. The Rebels moved their beds along and there was sufficient room for me to sleep between the mat covered hole and Don's bed. The mat and bearers over the hole would have held my weight but I did not want the mat to sag between the bearers. We turned in for the night and Horrie slept as usual on the foot of my bed.

I completed my scheme in mind before sleeping, if the idea failed we would have to think up another pretty good to take its place. Horrie was awake bright and early next morning and insisted on everyone else getting up also. He would give a friendly lick to any ear he could find and on being told to 'cut it out Horrie,' he turned his attention to the blanket and endeavoured to pull it off the sleeping Rebel. The cunning little blighter knows he can get away with almost anything groaned the molested Fitz. Immediately after breakfast I set out for the blockhouse near Ascalon.

These block houses were built at vantage points in the desert and they were used as strong posts in the event of any native uprising. Large square concrete buildings usually two or three stories high, they were said to be able to withstand a twelve month siege. Each structure had a high observation tower and could communicate with the next block house by visual signalling in the event of telephone lines being destroyed. Each block house was occupied by Englishmen of the Palestinian Police force.

Arriving at the block house near Ascalon I reached the entrance in the barbed wire fence that surrounded the building. Several police cars were parked alongside the driveway that ran from the entrance to the front of the building. Noticing a policeman busy in the task of washing the cars down I walked through the entrance and towards him.

He looked up from his job as I drew near. "What is it you want Aussie?" he asked. "Well," I answered, "I was wondering if you would do me a favour?" "Certainly, if I am able to," he replied. "Well..." I continued, "The position is this; sometime this morning I will be driving the skipper to Gaza. After dropping him there I will have the truck at my disposal for the remainder of the day providing that I don't return it to camp. A few cobbers and myself want to get into Tel Aviv for a last fling as we probably won't get the chance again; but here is the snag, the skipper always takes his little dog in the truck with him and I will be expected to return to camp after dropping him. I don't want to take the dog into Tel Aviv in case anyone pinches him out of the truck after we park it for the day in there, so I was wondering if I could leave him here and pick him up on our way home tonight." "You Aussie soldiers always seem to be AWL!" he laughed. I laughed also. "Well it's our last flutter in Palestine but I would not like to lose the skipper's dog through any fault of mine," I replied. "What time would you be returning?" he asked. "Probably about 9pm tonight," I replied.

"I'll be working here throughout the day and we will mind the dog for you, however when I am finished I will ask the duty man at the gate to hand him over when you arrive for the dog tonight. Will that suit you?" he informed me. "It certainly would!" I replied and telling him I would be back about 10.30, I thanked him.

Arriving back to camp I completed the next move in mind, I told Poppa to contact the Provost Sergeant and try and make arrangements for a truck to take Horrie and I over to the block house at Ascalon. Give it out everywhere that Horrie is being given to the Palestinian police for a mascot. Assuring the Rebels that everything was going according to plan they also started spreading the news. Poppa came back to the tent and advised a truck would be available at 10am.

I took Horrie on a lead to the Signal Office and told Big Jim and Captain Hindmarsh that the little dog was on his way. They were very sorry to see him go but agreed with me that it was better than destroying him, also they reckoned he would be in good hands and well looked after.

We made our way to the waiting truck, the Rebels and a few other lads had gathered to see the little dog off. The truck driver was Ron Ford, an old cobber, but he was not in the know about the scheme. One of the Regimental Provost coming over with us in the truck was not in the know either.

"Goodbye Horrie!" "Good luck little dog!" the Rebels called as we moved off.

On the way over to Ascalon, Horrie and I were in the back of the truck, the driver and the Provost in the front. The truck pulled up in front of the entrance and I noticed the policeman still washing the cars down. Alighting I told the other two that I won't be a moment and leading Horrie, I walked quickly over to the policeman in case he should come towards me and so into earshot of the two sitting in front of the truck. The policeman stopped work and said "Tie him up over there," indicating a horse trough.

I lead Horrie over to the trough and tied him up. "He will be alright here," he added.

Poor Horrie, as I walked back to the car being cleaned he barked after me asking me not to leave him.

Thanking the policeman and repeating that I would be back for the dog again at 9pm tonight I strode back to the truck with Horrie's bark ringing in my ears. As I drew alongside the truck I turned and called to the policeman "Take good care of him!" and he waved his arm in reply. "Okay, lets go" I said to the driver. After getting out of the truck back at camp both Ron and the Provost sympathised with me.

"Bad luck losing Horrie after all this time." I appeared none too cheerful and replied that he will have a good home anyway.

Poppa myself and the Rebels got the news around that at last old Horrie was gone. We appeared very miserable but kept pointing out to the sympathisers that the Palestinian police would take good care of him.

Quite unconsciously Big Jim, Captain Hindmarsh, Ron Ford and the Provost helped our carefully laid plan also and before long the news was an established fact all over the unit. Several of the troops were a bit surprised and asked why we didn't try to get him home. Captain Taylor, the pay Sergeant and Cal, an old cobber of Horrie's appeared quite upset, "Don't you think you could have at least tried to get Horrie home?" he asked. "I don't think we had a possible chance," I replied, "And poor old Horrie will be well cared for." Cal agreed about the well cared for part but I could tell from his manner that he thought we had let Horrie down. We were longing to let Horrie's firm friends into the secret but the motto was 'absolutely no chances.' Major Haupt told me he was sorry that we had lost our little dog.

Big Jim informed me it was the topic of conversation during the evening meal in the Officers mess. Everything was panning out beautifully, no one at all even suspected it was planned to smuggle Horrie home. Bill Cody one of the Signallers asked me "What's this I hear about Horrie being given to the Palestinian coppers?" "Yes that's right," I answered. "I'd have tried to get him home if you had given him to me." "No go Bill," I replied, "He would have been destroyed if he had been caught and as it is now he is in good hands." "Do you think he will be as well looked after?" he queried. "I should think so," I replied, "They are Englishmen you know." "I suppose so," he said, "But I would have given anything to see that little dog get home."

Dozens of troops enquired if we thought he would be okay. They were all assured that he would be but many were not happy about it. Although only a few remarked that we should have at least tried to get him home, many secretly thought that we had let the little dog down very badly. We could sense this feeling and the desire to tell them we were doing our best to get him home was very strong but 'no risks' and we kept the deceit up.

As the time approached for me to pick Horrie up again we discussed the best method of getting him back in the camp. I decided to take a towel with me and when back in camp lines I would carry Horrie under my arm, and if anyone was about I would drape the towel over my shoulder and make it appear as though I was returning from the showers that were not far down the road from our camp. It was also arranged that when I returned I was not to enter the tent if the small bucket that was used as a rubbish bin and placed outside of the entrance of the tent was missing. If any callers were inside I would know by the missing bucket.

I reached the block house on the tick of 9 o'clock, as I approached the entrance I whistled to Horrie. Horrie was apparently let loose, probably when my whistle was heard, and he came scampering out. He went through his usual song and dance in pleasure and not wasting any time we returned to camp. I picked him up and as there were quite a few lads moving about I concealed him with the towel. Cautiously I approached the tent. Okay, the bucket was in its place. The Rebels were there anxiously waiting for Horrie's arrival. The Gogg remained near the entrance of the tent to give warning if anyone came towards our tent. Horrie was very pleased and excited, his tail wagged like hell and his little mouth prepared to voice his pleasure also, but by gently and firmly holding his mouth closed and saying 'Sshh Sshh' he was kept quiet.

After letting go of his nose and jaw we would tell him he was a very good dog. 'Good dog Horrie': these words reassured him, but as soon as his mouth opened again the 'Sshh Sshh' was repeated by all. It was rather difficult and he could not understand for quite a while. He would cock his head on one side and look very concerned; 'here's a bloke trying to say he's pleased and they tell him to Shoosh', but by repeatedly informing him he was a good dog he at least understood to be quiet. Poor Horrie. As soon as he opened his mouth he was Shooshed.

We were about to try him out in the hole when the Gogg called 'Yow'. Don and Fitz rolled the mat back while I scrambled under a blanket, I made a tent with my knee and kept Horrie between them. Big Jim popped in and sat on Don's bed right alongside me. "What's up James you're in bed early?" he said, looking down at me on the floor. "I've got a touch of sand fly fever I think," I replied. "For goodness sake don't get sick at this stage of the game." "I'll be Jake I think," I replied, holding Horrie firmly between my legs and stroking his nose quietly with one hand. "I wonder how poor old Horrie is tonight" he asked.

I shut my eyes so I would not be able to see the faces of the Rebels. Don walked to the door of the tent and replied on the way, "I'll bet he is pretty miserable," and continued his way out of the tent. "What's up with Don?" asked Big Jim. Poppa saved the day, "Upset over Horrie," he replied. "Yes it's a bloody shame," said Big Jim. As Poppa mentioned Horrie's name there was a decided attempt at movement between my knees. "Sshh…" I said, then recovering "Let's not talk about it." "Well, I think I will turn in," said Poppa, rising to his feet The Rebels agreed they might as well also and after saying goodnight Poppa and Big Jim left the tent.

I removed the blanket but held on to Horrie while the Rebels nearly turned themselves inside out with surprised mirth. Don returned and said "For God's sake stop laughing this is serious." Poppa shook Big

Jim off and doubled back to the tent. "I'm getting too old to stand much of this," he laughed." "What do you think Big Jim would say if he knew about Horrie?" asked Feathers. "He'd be as right as rain but we would only be putting him on the spot," replied Poppa. The Rebels agreed. "I'll bet he will laugh when he does eventually find out," said Don.

We were amused at a mental picture of this also. The Gogg kept nit again and we rolled the matting back. While I was away getting Horrie, the Rebels had collected some old garments and made a bed for Horrie at the end of the hole. At the other end they had placed Horrie's water tin.

Putting Horrie down the hole... he thought it a new kind of game and tried to jump up but we Shooshed him again until in sheer disgust he lay down on the old clothes, 'Good dog, Good dog' we told him. We rolled the matting back in place. As the hole was then dark and we were unable to watch him by peering through the matting, Poppa produced a signal blackout torch and lighting it up we put it down the hole with Horrie; plenty more 'good dog' and 'shooshing' followed.

Horrie either understood or was thoroughly fed up as he prepared to go to sleep. Satisfied with the result, he was removed and allowed to sleep at the foot of my bed for the night although I attached a rope to his collar and the other end to my leg to prevent him going to the door of the tent to bark at any prowling wogs.

On reveille Horrie was placed in the hole. Poppa suggested I continue with the 'sand fly fever' for the day and remain in Don's bed which was a cane construction affair and alongside my own bed. I could then remain alongside Horrie and encourage him during the day. This was agreed by all to be good idea.

After the matting was put in position my equipment and gear was stacked on the head of what appeared to be a bed. Horrie was a bit restless during the morning and I had to remove the tin drinking dish as he bumped it once or twice and made a slight noise. I repeatedly told him he was a good dog and kept the Sshh up at regular intervals.

The approaching tent inspection was to be a very vital test, however on this the first day the tent was inspected by Captain Hindmarsh. The tents were inspected each day by the Orderly Officer and accompanied by the Orderly NCO, the inspection being to ensure that the tent was clean and tidy, equipment, etc stacked neatly at the head of each bed, Captain Hindmarsh accompanied by Ron Flett our Sergeant Major came into the tent and looked about. Seeing me in bed, Captain Hindmarsh enquired "What's the matter?" "A touch of sand fly fever," I replied.

This was not at all unusual as there was a fair bit of this complaint about. "Best take it easy for a bit," he replied. "Very good Sir," I replied, and they moved out. Horrie was particularly good all day and the only noise I heard was a dog's yawn. The Rebels brought my dinner into me, also some tucker for Horrie, the bones were kept until the night as the noise of him crunching them may be heard by anyone who popped into the tent.

While we were waiting for it to get dark after tea we discussed ways and means of his transportation to the ship. "We can rule the sea-kit bag out for a start," declared Don, "As the mob are familiar with this method." We all agreed. Although it was now very unlikely that anyone had any suspicions, we considered it best to try and think out a new method of carrying Horrie. "The universal kit bag is no good as they might be stacked down the hold," advised Feathers. There was only one method left, that being the pack that is carried on the back.

I suggested we try it out later that night. When darkness fell we took Horrie out of the hole and I put him under my arm again, having the towel handy to hide him if necessary. Don accompanied me and brought an empty pack and shoulder straps with him and also the very important little paper parcel containing some bones for Horrie. Feathers gave us the all clear and we left the tent by scrambling under the flap at the rear. We moved around the hill at the back of the tent and on reaching the vacated camp area where the Ack-Ack Regiment had been, I let Horrie down.

Poor Horrie, he was that pleased he hardly knew what to do with himself. Don and I sat down and let him rip. He was quite safe as he only scampered around where we were sitting. Just to please him we chased him around but as he barked a couple of times in excitement we retired again to sit and watch him. After he had exercised his little legs he came trotting back to us and Don opened the parcel of bones while Horrie watched the procedure with tail wagging interest. Poor old Horrie. After he had finished his bones we started the long task of training him to sit quietly in the pack. Don put the pack on and I lifted Horrie up and placed him in it, but at this stage I did not pull the flap over the top. Away we went around the old camping area, I walked close behind Don talking all the time to Horrie, "Good little dog... Sshh... Still Still."

Every now and then Don would stop and I would let Horrie out for a spell, sitting him on the ground we praised and patted him 'Good dog,' 'Good little Horrie,' 'Very smart pup.' Of course he just lapped this praise up, then I would swap places and Don would walk behind.

If Horrie moved at all we kept repeating 'still still'. He was not exactly comfortable as his weight on the bottom of the pack tended to make it fold in on him, but at the time it seemed the best we could do. After about one hours practice we pulled the flap over the top and fastened it to the two buckles on the front of the pack and once again we repeated the performance.

He did not object but before long his little nose had poked out of the top of the pack where the flap just covered the side, gently pushing his nose back inside we repeated the 'Good dog' praise.

The first night we spent only about five minute intervals in the covered pack but over the next few nights we increased the period until he was up to about two hours in the covered pack. The final lesson on the first night was to place the covered pack on the ground and Don and I sat alongside repeating 'good dog' and 'still still' when he moved.

Considering it sufficient for one night he was let out again and we took him for a long walk before returning to the tent.

As we approached the tent Don went on ahead while I remained at the rear of the tent holding Horrie in my arms. Presently I heard Don whistle okay in Morse code and Horrie and I entered the tent again from the rear. "Well how did the trial go?" inquired Feathers. "Okay," I replied, "I'm pretty sure he will be alright." We improved the pack a little by cutting a large round hole in the back of the pack, this we crisscrossed with string and Horrie was then able to get quite a lot of air. The hole could not be observed as the back of the person wearing the pack silhouetted the hole from sight. Horrie was permitted to sit at the foot of my bed but he was tied up to prevent any sudden dash on his part to the door of the tent. I remained near the bed so as to be able to cover him again with a blanket should anyone approach the tent.

Little did we think that another eight days had to be suffered by Horrie in the hole before we eventually moved. That night we discussed what we would do once we had gained the ship. Feathers suggested the latrine scheme that was approved but not necessary to adopt when we left Egypt for Greece. "But," replied Gordie, "It might be anything up to a month before we reach Australia." "What about the ship's crew?" suggested Fitz, "If we could make friends with them they may know of a place on the ship where we could hide him." This was a possibility and we decided to use the latrine idea until we got to know the crew and sized up their reaction to our plans. "There is nothing else for it but to keep him in the latrine accompanied by each of us in turn, if we suspect they won't play ball with us," I remarked. All the Rebels were quite willing to do this if necessary.

Poppa dropped in for a while and we informed him of the progress in the training and the suggested scheme. "The Sergeants may possibly have cabins and if this is so we maybe able to work a stunt," he informed us, "But in the meanwhile we had best stick to the latrine scheme until we see how things pan out," he declared. "Well we can't do much more about it until we actually get on the ship," replied Fitz. "Do you think there will be a kit inspection as we board the ship?" I enquired. "Most unlikely as we board," replied Poppa, "But once we get settled down it's a big possibility," he continued. "We best make sure and have something planned, just in case," I advised.

This problem proved a very tough nut to crack and it wasn't until the following day that the plan was formed. Before turning in, Poppa suggested that it was safe enough for me to continue to suffer from 'sand fly fever' for another couple of days just to make sure and keep Horrie's courage up.

Back into the hole went Horrie until daylight arrived. I was again laid up for the day and continued to shoosh Horrie and to repeatedly inform him that he was a good dog. The Rebels kept our tent extra clean and tidy so that there would be no close inspection or any room for complaint about the tent. Big Jim noticed this uncanny relapse on the part of the Rebels and he inquired if we were turning over a new leaf, 'Yes!' we grinned. During the day I lay for hours trying to think up some scheme of avoiding kit inspection and at last I got it and presented it for approval or otherwise to the Rebels after the evening meal.

This was the scheme. If a kit inspection was to be had, it was certain that the troops would be formed up in their ranks then the order given 'open order march'. After completing this movement the kit bags and packs, etc would be placed on the ground at the foot of the owner so that the gear could be inspected. If this took place it would probably be on the wharf, then after each had been inspected, the owner would pick up it up again and be directed up the gangway.

My idea was for the Rebels to occupy positions near me and as the inspection party got near I would drop down as though in a faint. Feathers and Don would immediately break ranks and go to my assistance but on reaching me I would weakly gain my feet with their assistance. Poppa was to notice the disturbance and advise Feathers and Don to help him up the gangway and Fitz was to move over to my gear and say to Poppa; 'I'll take his gear up' Poppa was to reply 'Yes, do that' and Fitz was to pick up the pack containing Horrie and carry it, not on his shoulders but by the top and follow us up the gangway. In this manner it was very likely that my gear would be forgotten.

Once on the ship the remainder was simple, Feathers and Don would inquire where I was to bunk down and escort me there. I would recover sufficiently enough so that it would not be necessary to take me to the Hospital Bay but to my bunk and there await the Rebels and so on to the latrine. Extra good they voted. Horrie was once again taken out for his exercise and training. Day after day and night after night the proceedings were kept up.

A few days before the move the expected order came out: 'All pets are to be disposed of.' But all was now arranged. After this order was given several lads remarked that it was probably just as well Horrie was given to the Palestinian police. Yes, we replied, the little wog dog is in good hands and will be well cared for. This may not have been Horrie's idea at the time but he accepted everything as being all in good faith. His behaviour now was perfect both in the hole under my bed and in the pack during his training. He would spend two hours without the slightest sign of movement.

The day before the actual move we were to have a trial move out of camp, each man carrying all his gear as he would do on the real move. This was to be a real test for Horrie's training and also of his stout little heart. We could have left him in the hole during this trial move but we decided to risk it and make sure all was well, the Rebels were to keep close to me and help cover up any movement on Horrie's part.

It was the day before the actual move and Horrie had completed eight days of solid training, he had survived every tent inspection although after my three days of 'sand fly fever' the Rebels took it in turn to have some mythical complaint and so remain in the tent alongside Horrie during the day.

All was set for the trial, the troops lined up, Horrie in the pack on my back and the Rebels close handy but we had forgotten one big factor; Horrie's training had all been under cover of darkness, also in the cool of the night, but now during the trial it was daylight and also very hot.

The first mistake was that the pack looked as though it was only half-filled and it collapsed in with nothing to hold the sides out, this made it a bit conspicuous and apart from that the sides collapsing in on Horrie made the poor little dog terribly hot, but only once did he move and 'Still' from Don behind me quietened him.

It could have easily been fatal but luck was with us and we completed the short march and regained our tent safely. As quickly as possible I got Horrie out and put him back in the hole, however this time I got down with him and the Rebels rolled the mat back in place.

Sitting down in the hole I quietly patted him and whispered to the panting pup. He had a heart like a lion and licked my hand to show he accepted all this and trusted us entirely. I laid him down on the old heap of clothes and gently stroked his head, he gave a sigh and dozed off to sleep.

All the Rebels had noticed that the pack needed some big improvement and we set to work right away, very shortly we had the perfect pack for the job. A strip of three ply wood exactly the size of the bottom of the pack was placed in position, two more strips were fitted up the sides. A small square hole was cut in the ends of the bottom board and a small protruding piece was left on the bottom end of each side strip, these protruding pieces fitted into the hole of each end of the bottom strip. This kept the pack out square at the bottom, the strip along the top rested on a slat packed just below the top end of each side strip. This top piece could be removed to allow Horrie to be put inside. It was a good fit and rested snugly on top keeping the top square. Horrie would have much more room and consequently be cooler.

I tried the pack on Don's back and added a further improvement by jamming a tightly rolled pair of socks behind Don's back and the bottom of the pack, this made a small space between the pack and Don's back and so allowing a flow of air.

That night Horrie was given a short try out and it proved excellent, in fact he could now move without it being so noticeable. When the pack was arranged as ordered a roll of blankets came over the top and down each side of the pack, and the tin hat was held between two straps in the centre of the pack at the rear when in carrying position. We were overjoyed at the result.

It was most unlikely that anyone would guess that the little dog was actually inside the pack. Horrie was also very pleased with the improvement and after being taken out he had more tail wags than on previous occasions. We did not stay out long that night as another problem had to be dealt with.

The next day the tents had to be taken down and packed into the trucks and the camp area cleaned up. This meant that the mat covering the hole had to be removed and another place found to hide Horrie during the next day. The Rebels had been working on this problem while Don and I gave Horrie his exercise and try out in the improved pack. "Well," declared Feathers, "We have got it worked out about filling the hole in." His suggestion was a good one, but it was going to take a lot of work and added risk to fill the hole up again by bucket arrangement. "We will leave the cane mat in place but cover the mat over with old newspapers then lightly cover the whole surface over with sand, it will then not be noticed." "Yes," I replied, "But Horrie won't be able to get any fresh air!" "Fitz has the answer to that," replied Feathers. Fitz suggested that as it was only for one day we could approach the Canteen Sgt. in charge of the canteen close to our area; it was a small wooden building and if he was a good sport he may keep Horrie out of sight in the building during the day, we could pick him up again at night.

This seemed a good bet and leaving Don to look after Horrie; Fitz, Feathers and myself went straight over to the canteen. The Sgt. proved a good sport and we let him into the secret. "Certainly," he replied, "I will keep him well out of anyone's sight and I wish you luck."

I arranged to take Horrie over to him before daylight the next morning. This I did and Horrie remained out of sight for the next day. Unfortunately I do not remember his name.

During the day we covered the hole as Feathers suggested and pulled down the tent for the last time in Palestine. There remained now only one small problem, we were to sleep that night in the open and move in the early hours of the morning by 'wog' buses to the Gaza railway station.

The problem was to keep Horrie out of sight until we moved off. This was very easy, as instead of sleeping with the rest of the troops just off the roadway, I left my gear with the Rebels and taking Horrie's pack with me, I lay down to wait some few hundred yards back from the troops. I retrieved Horrie from the canteen after dark and we waited in the selected spot until the troops started to get ready to embus. Putting Horrie in the pack I put it on and walked over and joined the Rebels.

The long journey back to Aussie was about to start and our carefully laid plan so far had worked smoothly. The bus journey to Gaza was without incident and we arrived at the railway station at about 3am. We had a considerable wait for the train as it did not arrive until about 9am. Horrie had to remain all this time in the pack. However it was not by far as bad as some of his earlier trials.

The group of Rebels moved down the platform a little from the remainder of the troops and after finding a cool place, I laid the pack on its flat after removing the tin hat. Horrie could now lay down and also see us through the string covered hole. I kept my felt hat handy and when any stranger came near us I covered the hole with my hat. Horrie was quite comfortable and our reassuring words to him kept his courage up.

When the train pulled up we were opposite the guards van and Don and I quickly seized the opportunity and hopped in with the guard, there was not sufficient room for the rest of the Rebels and they travelled in the carriage. The Arab guard was not so pleased at having his small compartment crowded by two soldiers and all their gear, but we were not going to let this worry us when we had the chance to let Horrie out of the pack during the train journey to El Kantara.

Waiting until the train got away, I then let Horrie out. The guard put on quite a turn when he saw Horrie. He spoke good English and he thoroughly understood what Don and I had to say during the first few minutes; for the remainder of the trip he was mostly intimidated and subdued 'Worthy Oriental Gentleman' that ever lived in the land of sun, sand, sore eyes, and sorrow.

Horrie also growled his warning that Don and I were fair dinkum apart from himself. We arrived at El Kantara on the Suez Canal without any further trouble. Putting Horrie back inside the pack we handed the guard a few hundred mils just to show our appreciation of his cooperation. Alighting from the train we were soon lost to his sight among the troops. A few hundred yards from the railway station there was a huge transit camp and here we received a meal before picking up the Egyptian train to take us to Port Tewfik.

Arriving at the transport camp Don removed my pack carefully in an upright position to enable Horrie to remain sitting inside the pack. The hole in the back of the pack had to be quickly covered up; this was managed by placing the remainder of our gear near the back of the pack and covering the top of the gap between the gear and the pack with Don's felt hat. However in spite of our care I noticed Captain Hindmarsh looking and laughing in our direction; he was always cheerful and jovial this popular OC of ours and maybe he was not the all seeing eye, 'who can tell': I can't.

After the meal we marched to the canal where a waiting punt took us across the Suez Canal and once again we entrained for Port Tewfik......

Pages 310 to 326 have been lost in time. After a restless night aboard the train, Horrie still in the pack. Arriving early Jim takes Horrie away from their camp to stretch his legs. Don and the Rebels have secured a tent with almost immediate embarkation. To much relief, Horrie's girl-friend Ishmee has gone all the way by truck from Syria with the Anti-Tank Regiment. The Rebels go over the plan to get Horrie on to the ship. The next morning, they march several miles in the desert sun, Horrie parched in the pack on Don's shoulders. At the half-way mark Jim gives Horrie a little water with his fingers. Finally they get to embark on a US ferry, now called West Point, and Poppa delightedly tells the company that there will be no kit inspection on the wharf. Imshee is not on their ship. The Rebels secure a large room, big enough for all of them, and friends Reg and Ron; who are simply amazed when Jim brings out Horrie from his pack. All agree they must keep quiet about Horrie and follow the plan to keep all away from knowledge of the wog dog. They work on a system of identifying WD (wog dog) knocks on the door to know friend or foe...:

p.326).......

and is hardly likely to be used by anyone not knowing its meaning. Don tried it out making the dots a lighter rap than the dashes. 'She'll do,' they agreed. "If any strange knocks on the door, the cove can pop Horrie into the shower room," suggested Gordie. But Don saw the danger here. "What if it is an unexpected inspection and the inspecting officer wants to see if the shower room is clean and tidy?" he asked. "Tell him someone is using the closet," replied Gordie. "Yes but what if he insists on seeing the room in spite of the bloke using it?" replied Feathers. "This is possible," I advised, "As you all know the word privacy has no connection with Private in the army." "Well then, what do you suggest, we can't use the blanket and tent method unless there are two in the cabin," remarked Fitz. "The only way I see out is to place Horrie in the pack," I replied. "Yes but you can't do that in a few seconds," replied Fitz.

We all agreed that this made it a bit awkward but Gordie found the right answer. "Replace Horrie in the pack and place it neatly with the gear on the bunk, give him a quick shoosh then open the door and appear as if you had been asleep; this will explain the delay in opening the door." 'That's the drill,' we all agreed, 'If there are two or more in the cabin use the blanket and tent method, if by yourself pop Horrie in the pack.' Don and I agreed to stay in the cabin for a while, the remainder drifted out to have a look around and see if they could get any news. Don and I lay down on our bunks after snibbing the door when the last Rebel had left the cabin. I patted Horrie gently on the head but he was dead to the world. "Horrie's all in," I informed Don. "No doubt," replied Don.

I didn't think a dog could willingly put up with what Horrie has. "Perhaps it would have been better if we had given him to the Palestinian police," I remarked. "What do you reckon Horrie would have said if he could talk?" replied Don. "Guess he would rather put up with anything than leave us," I answered. "Yes I'm sure of it," said Don. We hoped that Horrie's trials would now be over but he was yet to be given another test of spirit and courage.

The WD knock was rapped on the door and answering I was surprised to find Poppa waiting to be let in. "How did you know to rap WD?" I asked snibbing the door behind him. He informed me that Fitz had met him on deck and told him the cabin number and signal.

Poppa asked after Horrie and being shown where the little dog was fast asleep he declared; "That pup has more guts for his size than I thought possible." We certainly agreed. "I think a good half of his troubles are over now thank goodness," Don remarked. "We are not wasting any time," Poppa told us, "The ship pulls out tonight, no delay, no messing about for days and no convoy. One thing about the Yanks, they don't mess about," he added. "Do you know where we are going?" I enquired. "Not officially but pretty sure it's Aussie," he replied. The Rebels returned and Poppa let them in. "We're sure going to that little old Goddamn Australia buddy!" Fitz informed us. It seemed that everyone was quite sure but it was still only guess work.

We were to read the wonderful words on the ship noticeboard the next day, 'It is expected that this ship will arrive at Fremantle at 10am 26th March 1942' There was never a ship load of happier soldiers "Look at their faces" advised Poppa to me as we had read the words for ourselves. The news was around the ship in a flash but everyone had to see the noticeboard just to prove it for themselves. They were happy excited faces we saw coming away from the crowd gathered around the board. "Ask anyone to lend you ten bob now and they'd willingly give you their deferred pay!" laughed Poppa.

I returned to the cabin to enable the others to go up and see the good news for themselves. Later Poppa came down to let us know what was doing in the way of cabin inspection. Horrie had completely recovered from his ordeal and was his usual wagging self again. Even when the correct rap was given on the door Horrie was placed in one of the upper berths in order that he would not be seen by anyone in the passageway. "There will be no cabin inspection today but here is the routine from tomorrow onwards, the cabin will be inspected at about 10am, during the inspection one man will remain in the cabin but the remainder must be up on deck, and they are not allowed to return until 12 o'clock." Poppa advised us. "Well I will stay down during the mornings and be near to Horrie," I answered and this was agreed to. "The captain of the ship is the most popular man in the Red Sea," continued Poppa. "How is this?" asked Don. "They call him No Parade Kelly," advised Poppa, then explained that during the voyage there would be no parades at all on the ship. 'He'll do us,' we said. "Won't some of our parade officers be upset?" laughed Fitz. We laughed with him, this was right up our alley. "I think I'm going to like the Yanks," said the Gogg.

Big Jim came down to our cabin to see if we were all okay, his knock was the signal for Horrie's exit into the pack for the first time. When all was ready, Poppa answered the door. Big Jim was so pleased that he did not notice the delay in opening the door. "Suppose you blokes are happy now," he grinned. "How's that?" I asked. "Well you are going home!" he replied. "Oh that," I answered, "That's old stuff, knew about it way back in Syria." Big Jim grinned, "Wise guys heh?" "No just plain privates," Fitz replied. "Well what about a celebration when we land?" Big Jim suggested. "Okay let's make it a surprise party," I laughed. The Rebels guessed what the surprise was and laughed also. "What about doing some trick for us at the party?" Reg asked me. "Okay," I replied, "I'll do one especially for Big Jim but on one condition only…" "What's that?" enquired Big Jim. "That you won't tell anyone the trick." "Okay," he laughed, "But what is the trick." "I can't tell you now but it's called *Pack up your troubles*" Poppa nearly burst. "Well I don't know what all this is about," replied Big Jim, "But I'm intrigued." "You'll not only be intrigued but bewitched and bewildered!" laughed Poppa. After Big Jim had left us we let Horrie out again. "How would you like to be a little surprise dog Horrie?" Poppa asked him. It was quite okay for Horrie.

We decided then and there that if possible we would have a little celebration if we got Horrie home, we would invite Big Jim to attend and Horrie would be the main guest, he would be given a huge feed of the best steak we could buy and he was to receive his two stripes back again as a reward in recognition for his faithfulness, courage and devotion to the Rebels.

The next morning the Rebels had the cabin spic and span and shining like a new pin. As the time drew near for inspection I put Horrie in the pack and with the usual 'good dog, sshh' waited for the inspection, I felt quite confident that all would be well as Horrie could play his part alright. 'Stand by for ship's inspection' and into the cabin trooped the C.O. of our unit, one of the Ships Officers, the Company Commander and a few N.C.O's tossed in to make up good weight.

I had taken up position of attention near the head of my bunk which being the upper berth was above the line of sight of the inspection party. The cabin got a pretty good once over, even under the bunk was inspected but the Rebels had done a good job and they trooped out unable to complain, I waited until they had inspected the next cabin before closing the door and letting Horrie out: 'Very good dog Horrie,' but this was easy for him in comparison to his previous trials. The Rebels came down on the tick of 12 o'clock. 'Okay?' they enquired. "She's Jake," I replied. The next few days passed but there arose a very serious problem.

Horrie had been well trained during his period with the Rebel section and he would never dream of making his private arrangements anywhere near our tent, but he was now unable to leave the cabin and he was fighting against nature, it was the second day before we realised this.

I placed him in the shower room and remained in there with him for many hours hoping when he eventually gave up this worthy but unequal fight to be able to suggest to him the little sunken pit below the shower, but unknowingly I was defeating my purpose by remaining with him. 'Any luck?' enquired the Rebels who on the third day were very concerned. "No good at all," I replied.

Poor Horrie was beginning to look unwell. Fortunately I got the idea to put him in the shower room and close the door after him, after a period of half an hour I opened the door and the poor little pup came out very slowly and looking guilty and miserable; 'You poor little blighter but you are a good dog,' but he was still very unhappy. It was not until I left the salt water shower running and closed the door after him that he realised he was not going to be scolded. 'Good dog' and the little tail resumed its familiar wagging.

We were to receive a very nasty shock after lunch on the third day out from Tewfik. Poppa came in looking very serious. "What's up?" I enquired, noticing his serious face. "There has been a mistake made and this cabin really belongs to another unit, we have to get out and there is absolutely no chance of getting another cabin to yourselves now." "Struth, that would happen to us!" replied Gordie. "What is to becomes of us?" I asked. "There are several bunks empty in H.Q. area but they are only one's and two's," he replied, producing a piece of paper with cabin numbers on it and the number of empty bunks. "Well let's have a look around and see who is in these cabins," I said..

Poppa and I set off, leaving the Rebels with Horrie. The blokes in the cabins were all good coves but we were afraid the news that Horrie was on the ship might get around. One cabin contained all members of the Signal Platoon and this looked like the best bet for Horrie and I, as there was one bunk vacant. The inmates were all cobbers of Horrie's and if I could impress upon them the necessity of keeping the secret closely guarded all would be well.

They all turned out trumps and not a mention of Horrie was breathed by any during the trip. The lads in the cabin were Bill Arrowsmith, Bill Cody, one of Horrie's very close cobbers, 'Dar Dar' Davis, Syd Jordan, Jack Gardner, Gordon Baxter, Bill Martin, Bob Groll and myself.

Returning to the Rebels I inquired what they thought, they had located a cabin with four empty berths but this cabin was opposite a cabin used as a Company Orderly Room and was considered too dangerous. The fact that it had four empty berths showed its locality was not a popular one.

The Rebels offered to pop up to my cabin and continue to take it in turns while I got upstairs for a spell each day, but I was soon to find I had many willing helpers in the new cabin. I put Horrie back in the pack and the Rebels gave me a hand to move my gear. Entering the new cabin I snibbed the door behind me and you can imagine the surprise the Signallers got They could not believe their eyes. Horrie in his own tail wagging away, showed he remembered them all.

They readily agreed to the W.D. rap on the door and to help me carry out the scheme as we had done in the previous cabin, this new cabin being identical to the one I had to vacate. The Sigs also readily agreed to let me remain below each morning during the cabin inspection. The air inlet to this cabin was over Jack Gardener's bed and he permitted Horrie to sleep under the inlet on his bed, as it was starting to get uncomfortably hot and oppressive below deck. I told the Sigs the whole story and they all agreed that Horrie was as game as Ned Kelly. All continued to go well as far as keeping Horrie's presence a secret was concerned but approaching the line was almost unbearable in the closed cabin, but the Sigs stuck it out and in spite of the heat the cabin door always remained closed except at inspection time each morning.

Horrie felt the heat and although he showed no signs of complaining, he would lift his nose right up to the air inlet to get as much fresh air as possible. We could not do much to help him before cabin inspection, but after this was over I used to bathe him and sit him on the tiled floor of the shower room and fan him with a towel until he cooled down a little. As soon as I stopped fanning him his coat would become hot again and it was necessary to make him sopping wet every half hour, but he was as game as ever and always had a tail wag in reply to my efforts to cool him down.

After 12 o'clock the others were able to return to the cabin and Horrie had many willing friends to help cool him. This fanning and wetting continued for about six days but as we drew away from the line, it gradually became more bearable below deck. Part of the trouble was that the *West Point* had been designed for the Atlantic crossing and was consequently not the best in tropical areas.

At last it was over and Horrie's last severe trial was only a dog's bad dream. He brightened up and became full of beans again and his cheerful influence brightened up the cabin.

The days on deck were glorious and the troops relaxed and sun bathed, the Aussies and the Yanks got on very well and they soon learned the Aussie sport of 'two-up'. They were good gamblers and cheerful losers. Sports were organised to brighten the trip, boxing and wrestling bouts between the Aussies and Yanks were very popular and keen support was given to the competitors. A thorough feeling of good fellowship existed between the Aussies and Yanks.

We attended a church service given by the ship's Padre, it was bright and interesting. I remember part of the sermon that amused the Australians. It appeared that Moses had left some disciples in charge of some food which was pretty scarce at the time, however the disciples were told not to touch the food until Moses returned. However they slipped a bit and when Moses returned the food had vanished. It was the tone and the expression the Padre used that amused the Australians as he said that when Moses returned and found the fish had been eaten - 'Boy was he mad!'

We longed to take Horrie up on deck and let him scamper about in the sunshine but we stuck fast to the rule 'no risks' and at last the day arrived when we were to pull into Fremantle. We heard that Imshee was discovered just before arriving in Fremantle and disappeared.

Early after breakfast troops had taken up vantage points to be among the first to see Australian soil again and a little before 10am excited shouts and pointing fingers told their own story. Slowly but surely, out of the haze land became visible. Cheer after cheer rang out over the ship, excited Aussies shook each other's hands, voices were husky and eyes blurry, it was our own Australia and our home, there never could be anything as good. Poppa, Don and I silently watched this dream become a solid tangible thing. Poppa broke the silence by saying "If the Japs ever land in Aussie they had better bring a hell of a lot because they'll certainly need it!"

As the ship pulled in alongside the wharf the side of the ship was a highly wedged pack of cheering Australians, excited calls were exchanged between a few workers on the wharf and the Aussies; some one noticed a car with a charcoal burner attached behind, it was the first we had seen. Its owner was asked numerous questions: 'What is it, a bath heater?' The good humoured owner put a lighted match in somewhere and out shot a flame from the bath heater to roars of laughter from the troops. 'Lets go back to the Middle East, its too risky here!'

How clean and fresh the red roofed houses on the hill looked, 'Look, look, there's a pub!'; an old fashioned square two story wooden building, on the upstairs balcony we could see little white handkerchiefs fluttering. 'I'll bet it's called *The Bayview,*' laughed someone. We noticed a dog trotting contentedly up the road, a little more luck and perhaps Horrie may enjoy freedom like that old dog. "Keep your fingers crossed," said Don.

The West Australian soldiers were given four hours leave that night, we were to leave for Adelaide the following morning. Once again we were under way, a few more days and all being well Horrie would have his feet on Australian soil and would see daylight again after seventeen days. The last night on the ship all the Rebels and Poppa came to my cabin to discuss and plan the most important and vital effort to bring our carefully laid scheme to a happy ending. Horrie was excited and very pleased with himself, tail wags and licks of approval were given to all cabin inmates in reckless abandon. "Horrie seems confident anyway," remarked Feathers.

Poppa had found out that there would be no kit inspection on the ship, but there may possibly be one on the wharf, however he reckoned our best plan was to stick to the original fainting plan. I explained this to the Signallers. and they were very confident that it would succeed, but this time I would probably be bunged in an ambulance at the wharf. This was not much of a worry as by some means I would certainly be able to hop out with Horrie; anyway if I told the ambulance driver the scheme he would no doubt help. The Gogg gave me the address of his people. "Get Horrie there and he will be safe as a bank until you arrange to remove him. You could leave him there for good," he laughed. I thanked him but declined the latter. It was my ambition to see Horrie in the care of my Dad. "You know how we all feel about Horrie, Jim..." remarked Feathers, "But he is more your dog than anyone else's." "Well, I'll make you a promise," I replied, "First of all he will have the best home in the world and will receive more care and attention than ever we could give him. Secondly, I hope that someday he may take unto himself a bride and you can each have a pup if you wish. Don is to have first choice, Poppa second and the remainder of the Rebels in the order they choose." 'That's a definite promise?' they all asked. "Yes," I replied. "I'll call mine Horrie's son," remarked Don.

The next morning we arrived at Adelaide. After breakfast Don brought his gear up to my cabin in order that we would not get split up in the disembarkation. The gear was all packed and placed on the bunks and the time approached for the last cabin inspection, however this time all the inmates were allowed to remain in the cabin. Horrie was once again in the pack and a cabin full of crossed fingers awaited the last trial. Big Jim inspected the cabin by himself but it never ever looked so shiny and clean. Don and I stood in front of Horrie's pack, "Good show," remarked Big Jim and disappeared into the next cabin.

I shut and snibbed the door and we all breathed out, it was almost over. Lining up in single file we worked our way along the passageways until we reached the gangway. I was followed by Don, a few Signallers ahead of me and the remainder behind Don. As I reached the gangway I could have shouted for sheer joy, there was no inspection, the troops crossed the wharf and onto a waiting train. Almost in a dream I scrambled into a carriage, the Sigs ahead kept a window seat for me and before long Horrie gazed upon Australia through a criss-cross of string.

We were given a cup of tea and cakes by the Women's Welfare League before we moved off. As the train travelled into Adelaide the troops wildly cheered and called to all we could see but few knew anything about the movement of troops in those anxious days. I remember seeing a small notice on a fence: 'Welcome Home'. We alighted at the Adelaide station and amid many cheers and hand claps from the few that recognised returning troops, we marched to the Adelaide oval, here we were to have lunch before being taken to temporary billets.

Arriving there the Rebels came over to Don and I and we quietly stepped away behind a grandstand to let Horrie have a few minutes freedom and to watch our plans and dreams become a reality. Horrie stood quite still for a few minutes, his eyes were not yet accustomed to the daylight, then with a yelp of canine delight he investigated a fair dinkum Aussie gum tree.

His freedom was short lived as it was not yet all over. After lunch special trains took us to Burnside where we were to be billeted. A smiling Australian lady holding a bunch of papers in her hand took us to our allotted places; "There is room for two here," she informed Don and I and with a 'Good Luck' from the Rebels we waited inside the gate while she knocked on the door. "What if they don't like dogs?" whispered Don. "We will have to find out before Horrie is produced…" I replied, "If our luck is out I will get to work and locate some very old and good friends of mine here. I know they would love to keep Horrie until we can complete his Quarantine arrangements." "Would you come in please?" advised our escort. "This is Private Gill and Private Moody, Mrs Trezona." We were shown into a little room. "I hope you will be quite at home here," she said anxiously. Feeling a bit uncomfortable we assured her we would. "Unpack your things and join me in a cup of tea," she requested.

We put our gear in the room but were not yet game to let Horrie out, shutting the door after us and loud enough for our hostess to hear, we were called into the kitchen. "I hope you don't mind having tea with me here?" she asked. No we certainly didn't, it was a pleasant and friendly chat over that cup of tea and at last I got it out. "Are you fond of dogs?" I enquired. "Oh yes I adore them," she replied, a little surprised at the question. "Excuse us," said Don and I.

We reappeared in the kitchen carrying the pack upright between us, very soon our hostess was gazing at a little white enquiring head, two large brown eyes looked up hopefully from the pack. "The dear little war dog," she exclaimed. Horrie had captured another heart. That night when Mr. Trezona came home we told this friendly young couple some of Horrie's adventures and trials and before supper it was Ted and Mary, Don, Jim and Horrie. Horrie was well looked after and the following day we met the Rebels at the appointed parade ground, our broad grins told them all was well. I got a telegram away to my Dad:

HORRIE AND I ARRIVED SAFELY IN AUSTRALIA

The next few days were happy ones indeed. Horrie enjoyed his freedom in the large backyard. He was not yet allowed to be seen. Ted and Mary suggested a party for the Rebels and the surprise for Big Jim. Our unit was to be entertained at a ball at the Burnside Town Hall and Mary suggested a supper and party after the dance and so it was arranged.

It was a happy night for soldiers so long away from their own people and after the dance the Rebels and their escorts, including Big Jim, returned to the home of our new friends. The happy and gay chatter over supper was interrupted by Fitz asking for 'Attention Please!'

"It is my pleasure tonight to present to you all, especially Big Jim, the world's most uncanny magician and his able assistant, Dot and Dash!" Waving his hand towards Don and I, we acknowledged the hand claps. Fitz continued, "This trick has never ever been done before and probably will never be performed again. Dot and Dash have successfully blended all the magic of the mysterious East, all the skill of the cultivated West and all the determination of the sunny South, and I may add the North will be pulled into gear shortly also; the trick is known as *Pack up your troubles* Again we took the bow, I held up my hand for silence: "Ladies and Gentlemen and Poppa, before my rebellious partner and I perform this uncanny miracle I must ask you one and all to swear you will not repeat what you are about to witness for forty eight hours, this I ask you in all seriousness, do you all swear to it? Very well, watch closely..."

Don and I disappeared and returned carrying an oblong object covered with a white sheet, placing it in an upright position in the centre of the carpet, we asked all to gather round. When we were surrounded by the laughing folk I again asked for silence.

"As a very special honour I will now request our very good friend Big Jim to uncover the pack and trouble him to produce the 'Gem of the East'…"

Big Jim was laughingly thrust forward, he removed the sheet and unfastened the flap: "Horrie!" he exclaimed, lifting the little pup. The girls crowded round all laughing and patting Horrie, who passed me a scornful look. Big Jim called for silence, "Friends, this is one of the most pleasant surprises I have ever had, before I hand this little chap over, I am going to ask my friend James to tell you how his rebel friends and comrades performed this miracle." As he turned to me, I handed him a very small paper parcel and asked him to open it. Big Jim handed Horrie to our hostess and opened the parcel. "Rebel Section Attention!" then to Horrie, "Wog Dog you are from this moment reinstated to your former rank as Corporal" amid cheers and laughter.

The following day my brother, then a Sergeant Pilot stationed out of Adelaide, located me and after wagging his farewell to the Rebels and his new friends, Horrie, Bob and I completed the last leg of a successful journey. Horrie the Wog Dog is no longer a front line Digger as after nearly eighteen months service with the A.I.F. he has been honourably discharged.

We sadly miss the cheerful wog dog around camp but we are happy in the knowledge that the trials and dangers of the little wog dog are a thing of the past and he is happy and contented in the care of my Dad, a better man than I. We often look back over those days and none of us are sure if Big Jim's surprise that night was Fair Dinkum.

ADDENDUM

AUSTRALIAN MILITARY FORCES—NEW GUINEA FORCE

Headquarters

2/7 AUST INF BN
11 Jun 43

Dear MOODY,

      Yes. DIXON is still Adjt of the BN and he does recall having two stowaways on his hands for disposal.

      However, we would be most happy to have you back with the unit- this time for keeps- only wish you could have been with us during the flap. I'm sure you would have enjoyed it.

      The posn, at present, how we can assist you in effecting the transfer. I'll enclose an official letter with this, stating that transfer to this Bn is acceptable, providing it is concurred with by the unit. Should anything further be required of us, just drop a line and advise what other action you would like us to take.

      Regards to yourself and GILL,

      Sincerely Yours,

      Reginald Dixon Capt.

*Letter from Captain Dixon, "happy" to have Moody
back in the 2/7th Australian Infantry Battalion.*

Australian  Military Forces

TELEPHONE

Subject: TRANSFER

Please quote this Number when Replying

N/398

Address 2/7 AUST INF BN
11 Jun 43

VX 13091
PTE J.B. MOODY
2/1 MG BN

Ref your application for transfer and that of Pte GILL.

2. It is advised that application will have to be submitted through your parent unit.

3. Should transfer be concurred by them this letter can be shown as proof of our willingness to accept you both.

...............................Major

ADM COMD 2/7 AUST INF BN

Major Dunkley's response to Moody and Gill's request to transfer to their unit in New Guinea.

Angus & Robertson
June 1943
SYDNEY

J.B. Moody,
Private 2/1st Machine,
Gun Battalion, A.I.F.

Dear Mr Moody,

Mr Cousins, of Angus & Robertson Ltd., has handed me your M.S. re the Wog-dog, with the idea we both may make a book of it.

There undoubtedly is partial material for a good dog book in the M.S. Unfortunately, the material is not sufficient for a real book. The very least number of words a book should run to, is 60,000; really there should be no less than 70,000. Your M.S. runs to approximately 18,000 words. So that our problem is to find material for a further 40,000 concentrated words at least.

I have endeavoured to solve this by writing you a list of questions. Please read these over carefully first, then put the old memory back. Then answer each question (scribble it out in lead pencil) fully as you can. By the time you've got to the end you'll be surprised at how much more you know of Horrie than you previously thought you did. Then go over the questions again, and write the answers out fully for me.

If your mates are still with you, discuss the questions with them, a lot of memories are better than one. You'll find you'll be given a wealth of material to write down. Some of the lads also, will know stories of Horrie that have escaped your notice, or memory.

Any question that brings up some other incident not mentioned in the M.S., then write down that incident also. In this way I'm quite sure we'll get enough material for what should prove a jolly good book. Don't be afraid of answering any questions very fully, or of adding more copy, so long as you send along "meat".

Cheerio. And here's wishing the forthcoming book every success.

Sincerely,

J. L. Idriess

Moody's first letter from Idriess from Angus & Robertsons in June 1943.

QUESTIONS.

A. Please describe, in all detail that you remember, the dog when he first joined up. Colour, size, anything at all about him. And, as he later developed any particular characteristics whatever. As described now, he is but a "shadow dog". Hence, it is very neces ary that any habit, any peculariaty, any characteristics should be described, both on adoption and as he grew, so that a picture of a "live" dog can be quickly built up in the readers mind.

I understand that the dog may be in Sydney. If so, I'd like the address and a chance to go out and see him.

Also, re photos. Any photos of him, together with interesting photos of the battalions adventures, would help the book immensely. *P.S. Mr Cous-n has since told me he already has the photo's.*

B. Who is Big Jim Hewitt? He is only mentioned in the very last line, yet apparently he had quite a lot to do with the dog.

As you read the questions you will repeatedly see "give names of cobbers, scraps of conversation etc. This will all help to build up the book. Not only the dog, but the men closely associated with him must be "living characters" for the book to live.

1. Was it on an expedition to the old Roman city that you found Horrie? What were the names of your companions? Do you remember any scraps of conversation re the dog? For instance, who suggested name of Wog-dog? Any particular reason for the name Horrie?

2. Dog covered his feet with sand. Who suggested "you can scarcely blame him"? (names and scraps of conversation always make an incident more interesting) Who was the spark suggested he might be an Italian dog?

3. Who were your tent-mates who took most interest in the dog?

4. While on route marches, the Arab urchins back chat, especially in regard to the dog would win a laugh from the reader. Slip in as many witty remarks or incidents, occurring at any time, or on any occasion, as you can possibly remember.

5. When about to move from Egypt, the question was "What about Horrie." Please think up a few scraps of conversation, any suggestions the boys made etc. It will make the story more personal and convincing. Give names whenever you remember. Also any little details in training Horrie to the kit bag.

6. Any amusing incidents during the train trip?

7. "One of the boys called Yow", to what does this refer?

8. Re ships crew and their dog. A few personal incidents about members of the crew, their dog, and still more of Horrie, aboard ship would add to interest.

9. The sea sickness incident is quite good. Any more cheery little touches would be appreciated — by the reader anyway.

10. When you made a life jacket for Horrie, what were names of cobbers who lent a hand, or took an interest? Throughout the entire book please add these

The first page of 63 questions from Idriess to Moody to try and encourage Moody to better reveal the Tale.

Pte J Moody
"C" Coy
2/1 M/G Bn A.I.F. 27 July.

Dear Mr Idriess

I am forwarding the enclosed 124 pages
on the instalment plan, it being rather
inconvient for me to keep it until I
have answered all your questions. As you
know this country you will appreciate
the difficulty in keeping things dry.
I will continue with the remaining quest
ions and hope to get time to finish
them very soon. Would appreciate ack
on receipt of 124 pages, also if any meat
is obtainable from some.

Sincerely J B Moody.

PS. Paper of any kind is as scarce
as my correctly spelt words up here. JM

Letter from Moody to Idriess July 1943.

55 Meadow St
East St Kilda
28th Feb.

Dear Mr Idriess
Received your letter of the 7th Feb
glad you appear to be satisfied with
the first chapter and trust you will
be able to continue the good work
through out the book. At the
moment am at home on leave, but
I expect to be in Sydney about the
20th March, if there is anything I can
do, or if you so wish it, I will
contact you in Sydney. If you desire
this, let's know before the 15th March,
the above address will find me.
              Cheerio
                  Jim Moody.

Letter from Moody to Idriess February 1944.

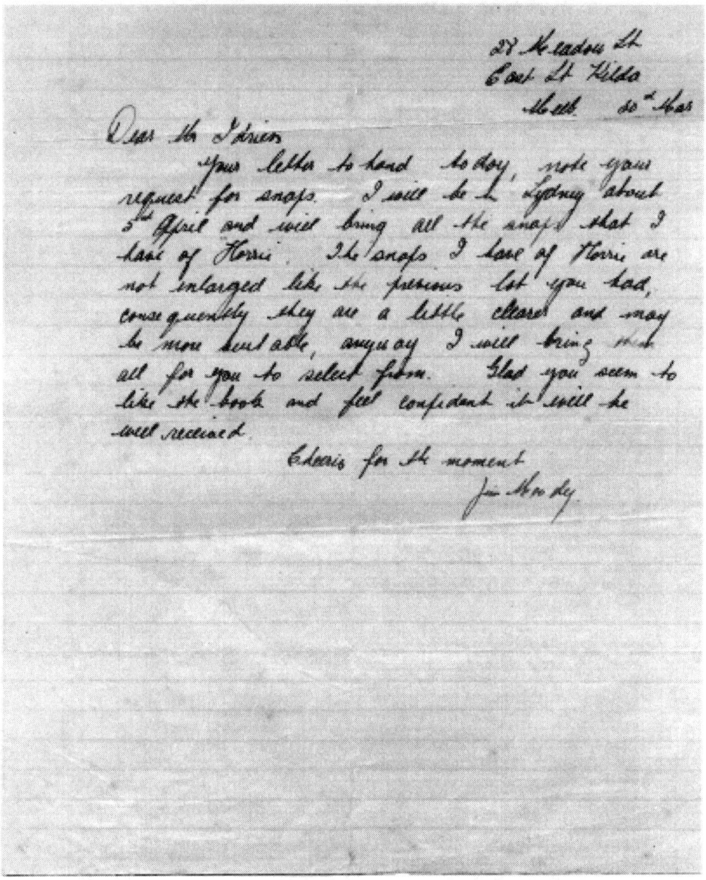

28 Meadow St
East St Kilda
Melb 20th Mar

Dear Mr Idriess

Your letter to hand today, note your request for snaps. I will be in Sydney about 5th April and will bring all the snaps that I have of Horrie. The snaps I have of Horrie are not enlarged like the previous lot you had, consequently they are a little clearer and may be more suitable, anyway I will bring them all for you to select from. Glad you seem to like the book and feel confident it will be well received.

Cheerio for the moment

Jim Moody.

Letter from Moody to Idriess 20 March 1944.

Veteran: Honorary
member of the Melbourne
RSL, Horrie, who has been
in five campaigns, poses with
his owner, Jim Moody, discharged AIF, and Sergt.
Roy Brooker.

The first photograph of Moody with Horrie February 1945.

Quarantine Act 1908.

SEIZURE FORM.

To _J. C. Moody_ 28 Silver St., St. Peters.

The person having possession of any goods, animal, or plant subject to Quarantine.

I HEREBY SEIZE the Goods enumerated and described below, and which I have marked as shown below :—

Kind and Number of Goods.	Description and Brands or Marks.	Seizure Mark.
1 Dog	Egyptian Terrier	

12 . 3 . √ʃ¹⁹ .

M. King
Officer.

C.7699.

Letter of Seizure of one Egyptian Terrier!

HORRIE
THE WOG-DOG
The Original Tail

ION IDRIESS

The final stage of Moody's Tale, published in 1945, now in its
eighth edition.